NIST Special Publication 260-131, 2006 Ed.

Standard Reference Materials®

The Certification of 100 mm Diameter Silicon Resistivity SRMs 2541 Through 2547 Using Dual-Configuration Four-Point Probe Measurements, 2006 Edition

James R. Ehrstein*
Semiconductor Electronics Division
Electronics and Electrical Engineering Laboratory

M. Carroll Croarkin*
Hung Kung Liu
Statistical Engineering Division
Information Technology Laboratory
* Retired

National Institute of Standards and Technology
Gaithersburg, MD 20899

(Supercedes NIST Special Publication 260-131, 1999 Ed., June 1999)

February 2006

U.S. Department of Commerce
Carlos M. Gutierrez, Secretary

Technology Administration
Under Secretary of Commerce for Technology, William Jeffrey, (acting as)

National Institute of Standards and Technology
William Jeffrey, Director

Table of Contents

Table of Contents (cont'd.)

List of Figures

List of Tables

Standard Reference Materials:
The Certification of 100mm Resistivity SRMs
2541 through 2547 using Dual-Configuration Four-Point Probe Measurements,
2006 Edition

by

James R. Ehrstein
Semiconductor Electronics Division, EEEL

and

M. Carroll Croarkin and Hung Kung Liu
Statistical Engineering Division, ITL

This report documents the selection of material, the certification procedure and its control, and the analysis of measurement uncertainty for a family of improved Standard Reference Materials (SRMs) for sheet resistance and resistivity of silicon wafers, SRMs 2541 through 2547, covering the resistivity range 0.01 • •cm through 200 • •cm. These SRMs, made from 100 mm diameter silicon, replace previous SRM sets 1521 through 1523, which used 50.8 mm (2 in) diameter silicon at the same nominal resistivity levels. This revised report replaces both the original 1997 report and a 1999 update. It contains three new appendices: 10, 11, and 12 which summarize H.-K. Liu's statistical reports of analysis of second batch certifications for SRMs 2541, 2543 and 2544 as well as an appendix 13 that details the SRM serial numbers that were part of those second batch certifications. This revision also includes updates to tables 10 through 15 to include summaries of the uncertainty component results from those "second-batch" certifications.

The certification of the improved SRMs uses a dual-configuration four-point probe procedure rather than the single-configuration procedure of ASTM F84 [1], as used for previous SRMs. The new SRMs offer better handling compatibility with current user instrumentation, better uniformity of wafer thickness and of resistivity, more extensive spatial characterization of the near-center wafer resisivity, and reduced measurement uncertainty.

The general procedures for the certification measurements, the control of the certification process, and the analysis of the results are based on experience gained from numerous preliminary experiments that allowed evaluation of the importance and relative magnitude of many possible measurement effects. The validity and effectiveness of the resulting certification and control procedures were tested during the analysis of results from the first of the SRMs to be certified, that at 200 • •cm. The body of this report details the background and principles of the certification process and the approach to analyzing the experimental data needed to calculate the uncertainty of the certified values. This report details the evaluation of underlying Type B components of uncertainty that apply to all SRM levels.

Additional Type A components, derived from statistical analyses of the actual certification data, are done individually for each SRM level and are reported in separate appendices for each of the SRMs.

Key Words: four-point probe; resisitivity; semiconductor; silicon; SRM; standards

INTRODUCTION

This Special Publication summarizes the certification procedure for a new generation of silicon resistivity Standard Reference Materials (SRMs) 2541 through 2547. It includes, in individual appendices, the analysis of the associated uncertainty levels calculated from the certification data for each of the resistivity levels.

Previous Resistivity SRMs

For a number of years, the Semiconductor Electronics Division of the National Institute of Standards and Technology has issued three sets of silicon resistivity SRMs. These sets, designated 1521, 1522, and 1523, contained two, three, and two wafers, respectively, of 50.8 mm (2 in) diameter silicon with the resistivity values in each set having been chosen to serve a particular application need in the silicon semiconductor industry. The generic purpose of each of these sets was to allow a user to verify the performance of a four-point probe* test instrument, or to calibrate the output of a noncontact eddy current conductance-measuring instrument. The resistivity values of these SRMs ranged from about 0.01 $\Omega \cdot$cm to about 200 $\Omega \cdot$cm. More than 1300 sets of these SRMs have been certified and sold worldwide. Each wafer in each set was certified for resistivity using a four-point probe following the measurement procedure of ASTM Method F84 [1]. This procedure is also referred to as a "single-configuration" four-probe procedure in the remainder of this report.

Improved Resistivity SRMs

After several years of exploratory work, the Semiconductor Electronics Division is issuing improved SRMs at the same resistivity levels as in the previous sets, but having four salient upgraded features:

1. The new SRMs are wafers of 100 mm diameter silicon which enables better compatibility with present generation user instrumentation.

---

* In the remainder of this report, the term "four-point probe" is used when referring to the probe itself. The term "four-probe" is used when referring to the measurement process.

2. They are fabricated from silicon with improved uniformity of resistivity and thickness. This will reduce ambiguities of interpretation related to measurement sampling volume, and it will improve transferability of the certified value to the end user.

3. They are certified with a modification of the original certification procedure. This modified procedure is referred to as "dual-configuration" or "configuration-switched" four-probe measurements and is implemented on most commercial four-point probe instruments that are automated for thin-film sheet resistance mapping. Tests at NIST have shown there is also a significant reduction of uncertainty when using this procedure for measuring bulk silicon wafers.

4. Measurements and analysis are provided at the wafer center, as was done with the original SRMs, and also around two small circles with sizes related to the requirements of commercial resistivity-measuring instrumentation. These additional data serve to characterize the small nonuniformities in resistivity that are present even in these wafers.

While these improved SRMs are issued singly, rather than in sets, it is strongly recommended that for all purposes of calibration or testing of instrument linearity, SRMs at two or more resistivity levels be used, with the values being chosen according to the user's application needs.

A major goal of these SRMs has been to meet or exceed the requirements set forth at the SEMATECH Workshop on Silicon Materials for Mega-IC Applications [2]: **"That layer resistivity measurements be improved to an accuracy of 1 % and repeatability of 0.5 % and that NIST provide the SRMs required for such measurements."**

1. CERTIFICATION OF IMPROVED RESISTIVITY SRMs

1.1 General Comments

While it may seem trivial to generate silicon resistivity standards that far exceed the SEMATECH Mega-IC Workshop requirements for precision and accuracy, this is not the case. Silicon is a semiconductor, nonuniform in resistivity in both lateral and vertical directions, unpassivated for use as an SRM, that can be measured with a four-point probe and, therefore, subject to possible surface effects due to storage and handling environments that can modify the near-surface resistivity. A lapped surface is used on SRM wafers to increase surface recombination velocity, to improve the quality of contact with the spring-loaded probe tips, and to improve the long-term stability of measured resistivity by reducing the susceptibility to changing surface conditions. This, in turn, introduces compromises in terms of near-surface damage, and of the definition and measurement of wafer thickness. Four-point probes are used for certification measurements, and the probes are subject to wear and to changes in contact quality and performance that may be either gradual or rather sudden. Despite a number of efforts, no simple characteristic of a probe pin has been identified that is

3

a clear indicator of how that pin will contribute to the quantitative performance of a given four-point probe. It has been found that measurement precision with a single probe head, as well as measurement variability among probe heads, are functions (among other things) of resistivity, conductivity type, specimen surface preparation, environmental conditions, and present condition of the probe pins themselves.

It is possible, using a technique such as the van der Pauw procedure [3] with contacts bonded to the perimeter of a polished wafer and with measurements done in an ambient capable of controlling wafer surface charge, to eliminate many of the concerns related to measurements with mechanical probe contacts. It might be possible in this way to eliminate or reduce noticeably a number of sources of measurement variability. Such measurements would then have a lower uncertainty than those made by four-point probe on a lapped wafer and might well provide the best estimate of overall volume average resistivity for an entire silicon wafer. However, this would probably not be particularly useful for calibrating or verifying the performance of instruments used in production environments if the measurements required a special ambient for measurement or if the full-wafer average resistivity did not bear a clear relationship to the localized (small area) value measured by the production test instruments.

An important distinction needs to be made. The principal objective of these SRMs is not to provide the best value of the volume resistivity of the silicon wafer itself, but to use the SRM wafer to help define and transfer a functional resistivity/sheet resistance measurement scale to users of common instrumentation in various parts of the semiconductor industry. Currently, most such equipment is based on four-probe dc resistance or on eddy current measurements and has spatial sampling volumes on the centimeter scale. There is no known analytic expression for the exact volume weighting of measurements by a four-point probe or by an eddy current tester with a ferrite core. As a result, it is not possible to guarantee perfect equivalence between four-probe and eddy current instruments for specimens with various and arbitrary patterns of resistivity nonuniformity. Nevertheless, resistivity SRMs based on lapped silicon wafers with certification measurements by four-point probe, particularly when done with a well-controlled measurement system used in the dual-configuration mode, and with measurements in well-specified locations on the SRM wafer, offer the user community several significant benefits. These are: stable SRM artifacts, measurement sampling volume generally comparable to that of the user's instrumentation, and certified measurement precision and resolution that more than meets the requirements of the semiconductor industry. *Thus, in developing these SRMs, the interest is not so much in what the true bulk resistivity of each silicon wafer is, but rather in how the measurement values on these wafers behave as a function of measurement conditions, and how the SRMs transfer between NIST and the user community.*

There are two principal reasons for preferring the dual-configuration implementation of four-probe measurements for the SRM certification. First, the probe-to-probe differences are reduced noticeably compared to those that exist when using the single-configuration (ASTM) procedure; such differences are generally only several tenths of a percent, but make it difficult to reach or exceed the accuracy goals in the SEMATECH Mega-IC Workshop report.

Second, the scatter, or random error, is reduced in a set of measurements taken with any given probe. Both improvements are interpreted as being due to the ability of dual-configuration measurements to correct more exactly for the true electrical probe separations than can be done with the auxiliary optical and mechanical separation measurements required by the ASTM Method, in combination with single-configuration electrical data.

For some time, it was common among users of the technique to speak of configuration-switched rather than dual-configuration four-probe measurements. The term dual configuration is used in this report when the term is written out in order to reinforce the operational difference from the ASTM, or single-configuration, procedure.

The following sections discuss the details of the procedures used for certification, and its control, as well as the manner of analyzing, and reporting the results. They also give a brief description of the components of measurement uncertainty in relation to the equation used to calculate the reported results from the raw data. Section 5 discusses the evaluation of uncertainty in more detail, but organizes the discussion according to whether the various contributions are evaluated by ISO Type A or Type B evaluation procedures (see 1.3).

1.2 Resistivity Standards vs. Sheet Resistance Standards

This SRM is called a "resistivity" standard, and much of this report and the SRM certificate focus on describing it and analyzing the measurements in terms of a resistivity value. This is done primarily as a concession to customary terminology and conceptualization in the semiconductor industry wherein "sheet resistance" is a property associated almost exclusively with a thin film of conducting material rather than with a substrate wafer. However, these SRM wafers do have sheet resistance values associated with them (resistivity divided by thickness), and moreover, the functional need of most user instrumentation is actually for calibration or verification of a (sheet) resistance scale, and not of a resistivity scale.

This distinction is not simply one of semantics. There is an actual benefit to the user from treating the SRMs as sheet resistance reference artifacts. To obtain resistivity values for a silicon wafer, it is necessary to know the wafer's thickness. But when silicon wafers are lapped in order to improve their stability as electrical reference standards, the surface texture compromises the possibility of a wafer having a single, unique wafer thickness. The determination of the wafer's resistivity value is therefore poorer than that of its sheet resistance value because of the added uncertainty due to thickness. Thus, each of the SRM wafers has a somewhat larger relative uncertainty of resistivity than it does for sheet resistance.

Further, if the user employs these SRMs to establish a scale for resistivity but uses an independent measurement of thickness such as from a capacitive- or sonic-gauge, then the user must add yet another component of uncertainty to the transfer process. The reason is that these other instrument types are different in operating principle from that of the contacting electronic-micrometer which is used at NIST for the determination of SRM wafer thicknesses. Therefore, they are not likely to give the same functional value of wafer thickness that is reported on the SRM certificate, and an additional measurement error is incurred in establishing a resistivity scale. However, sheet resistance values do not depend on measured thickness value, and transfer of SRM (sheet) resistance values are unaffected by this consideration. It is therefore recommended: 1) that these SRMs be used as **sheet resistance standards** whenever possible and 2) that the thickness value given on the certificate be used whenever a resistivity value is needed.

[**Note**: Thickness values for lapped surface wafers typical of those being used for these SRMs have been found to be about 0.5 % smaller when measured with a capacitance gauge than when measured with an electronic-micrometer. These capacitance-gauge thickness values are probably closer to the actual thickness of the electrically conducting portion of the wafer (beneath the lapped texture) than are those from the electronic-micrometer. However, for the purposes of SRM certification, it is easier to establish traceability of thickness scale to dimensional standards when using an electronic-micrometer.]

1.3 Traditional Description of Uncertainty and the ISO Formulation

Measurement uncertainty for these SRMs is reported in conformance with guidelines formulated by the International Standards Organization, ISO [4, 5]. Sources of uncertainty are classified as Type A or Type B according to whether their values are estimated from repeated measurements (Type A), or are inferred in another manner (Type B). A variance is calculated, or estimated, for each contribution to the uncertainty of the measured value; a sum of variances is then done separately for Type A and Type B evaluations. The square root of the sum of the Type A and Type B variances is calculated and is called the combined standard uncertainty, u_c. A quantity called the expanded uncertainty, U, is calculated by multiplying the standard uncertainty by a coverage factor, k. This factor can often be taken from the Student t tables to give a stated coverage, say 95 %, if the degrees of freedom can be calculated. The effective degrees of freedom in the analyses of each of the SRM levels are sufficiently large, typically 60 or more, that a factor of k = 2 gives a coverage of 95 %.

Where sources of uncertainty for this SRM are estimated from other than repeated measurements, it is generally assumed that the affected measurements come from a rectangular distribution, the limits of which are the values that would have been assumed as the maximum systematic error for that quantity. For a rectangular distribution, the variance is the half-width divided by $\sqrt{3}$. There is not always a one-to-one correspondence between the categorization of traditional sources of measurement error as being random or systematic and the uncertainty components determined by Type A or Type B evaluation procedures.

1.4 Acquisition and Characteristics of Silicon Wafers for the SRMs

Wafers at all SRM resistivity levels were bought, having been already cut, etched, and lapped by the supplier. The supplier for each of the resistivity levels is identified on the SRM certificate. All wafers are nominally 625 µm thick. The perimeters of all wafers were contoured to reduce breakage; a single primary orientation flat was ground onto all crystals prior to slicing. The supplier of the wafers for the three lowest resistivity levels, 0.01 Ω·cm, 0.1 Ω·cm, and 1 Ω·cm, used a laser marking technique to engrave a unique wafer identification into each wafer just above this flat; the suppliers of the four highest levels did not offer such a marking process.

Wafers at the three lowest resistivity levels are from (100) boron-doped Czochralski-process (Cz) silicon crystals, while wafers at the four highest levels are from (111) crystals phosphorus-doped by the neutron-transmutation doping (NTD) process. These combinations have been found to be appropriate for meeting the goal of high uniformity of resistivity across a resulting wafer.

The suppliers[**] selected (Recticon Inc. for the three lowest resistivity levels, Wacker Siltronic for the middle level, and Topsil Semiconductor Materials A/S for the three highest levels) specialize in the types of growth processes listed. Preliminary batches of wafers from each supplier were evaluated for thickness and resistivity uniformity. These evaluations indicated a high degree of likelihood of total thickness variation being less than 1 µm over the wafer surface and of resistivity uniformity being 1 % or better within the central 50 mm diameter of the wafers. These levels of uniformity are not guaranteed, however.

1.5 Measurement Concerns and Control of the Certification Procedure

Extensive preliminary testing was done to reach a reasonable optimization of the wafer preparation and test conditions, to minimize or eliminate effects that would degrade the certification uncertainty, and to estimate the relative importance of the various known remaining effects. These tests then led to the design of several experimental control procedures to monitor and evaluate possible changes in probes, wafers, or instrumentation during the certification.

The following sources of experimental variability and possible error were identified and are listed along with the procedure that was developed to minimize their effect and to estimate their value.

[**]Certain commercial equipment, instruments, or materials are identified in this report to specify adequately the experimental procedure. Such identification does not imply recommendation or endorsement by the National Institute of Standards and Technology, nor does it imply that the materials or equipment identified are necessarily the best available for the purpose.

1. Short-term imprecision (repeatability of measurements taken within a period of minutes in a small, uniform region of material) is believed to be controlled by probe contact fluctuations and electronics noise; it is minimized by using the dual-configuration procedure and choosing a probe with low noise. Short-term imprecision is evaluated from data at the centers of the certified wafers, as well as from all wafers used in the control procedures.

2. Longer-term imprecision (the ability to reproduce an average value at a fixed point on a wafer over a period of days or weeks) is related to changes in the measurement environment, e.g., power-line conditions, electromagnetic interference, or humidity. No measurements are taken at a relative humidity above 50 %, and residual long-term imprecision can be evaluated from the control experiments.

3. Probe-to-probe differences in measured value have been seen to exist. Although small (0.1 %, or less), it is necessary to identify and select for certification a probe with low bias. This is done through the design of one of the control experiments. Residual offset for the selected probe is estimated through analysis of this control experiment data, and a correction applied to the measured results if the offset is statistically significant.

4. Possible drift of the measurement process with time, whether due to changes in the probe used for certification, the wafers being tested, or to strong changes in the measurement environment. Drift can be estimated from the design of one of the control experiments.

5. Possible dependence of the measured resistivity value on the current value is controlled by a very tight procedure for selecting the current level for each SRM wafer.

6. Wafer nonuniformity effects on the certified values of resistivity are minimized by using very high uniformity wafers and by using a tightly controlled procedure for selecting the measurement locations.

7. Error related to the temperature dependence of resistivity value is controlled by measuring the temperature of the wafer stage and applying a correction for the difference between ambient and a reference temperature of 23 °C for each line of measured data. An estimate is made of the uncertainty of the temperature correction, and this estimate is part of the Type B standard uncertainty.

8. Possible error related to the accuracy of the measurement current supply and the digital voltmeter (DVM) are minimized by using standard resistors to measure the current value and by using the same scale of the DVM for measurement of both

wafer voltage and standard resistor voltage drops. Residual uncertainty related to the voltage measurements is estimated by Type B procedures.

9. Possible error related to the accuracy of the thickness measurement tool is minimized by instrument checks, several times a day, on NIST-traceable gauge blocks of thicknesses very close to those of the wafers. All wafers with a total indicated runout in excess of 1 μm over a nine-point thickness measurement pattern are rejected. Residual thickness measurement uncertainty is estimated by Type B procedures.

Accumulated probe damage in the wafers should not be detectable within the duration of the tests being performed. Previous tests on approximately a dozen wafers similar to these SRMs showed no effect out to 3000 probings for most wafers. However, a few wafers in those tests did show noticeable shifts (about 5 %) in average resistivity and greatly reduced measurement precision after about 1500 probings.

2. CERTIFICATION PROCEDURE

To minimize the effects of test instrument performance on measurement accuracy, a high degree of reliance is placed on ratioing techniques for both wafer thickness and electrical measurements, with the instruments being checked against precision calibration standards. Thus, the instrument used for wafer thickness measurement is regularly verified against gauge blocks having thicknesses very close to those of the SRM wafers, and measurements of the voltage drops across the silicon wafer and the standard resistor are read on the same scale of the same digital voltmeter. The standard resistors employed for monitoring the current serve as the primary reference point for all electrical measurement values.

2.1 Wafer Thickness Screening and Thickness Measurement

Preliminary screening with a capacitance-type thickness instrument of a small random selection of wafers from each of the actual SRM batches showed typical within-wafer thickness variation to be 0.2 μm, or less, for the central region where four-probe measurements are taken. This is noticeably better than the uniformity requirement of 1 % (which would be about 6.2 μm for the SRM wafers), as required by ASTM F84 for referee resistivity measurements.

For the certification procedure, thickness measurements of each wafer are taken on a three-row by three-column grid with a distance of 19 mm between the wafer center and the corners (Fig. 1). (The locations are approximate since the wafers are positioned manually.) This nine-site sampling gives a reasonable measure of the thickness and its variation in the area used for electrical measurements. Because the small contact area of the electronic-micrometer is more sensitive to local fluctuations due to variations in lapped surface texture, there is more

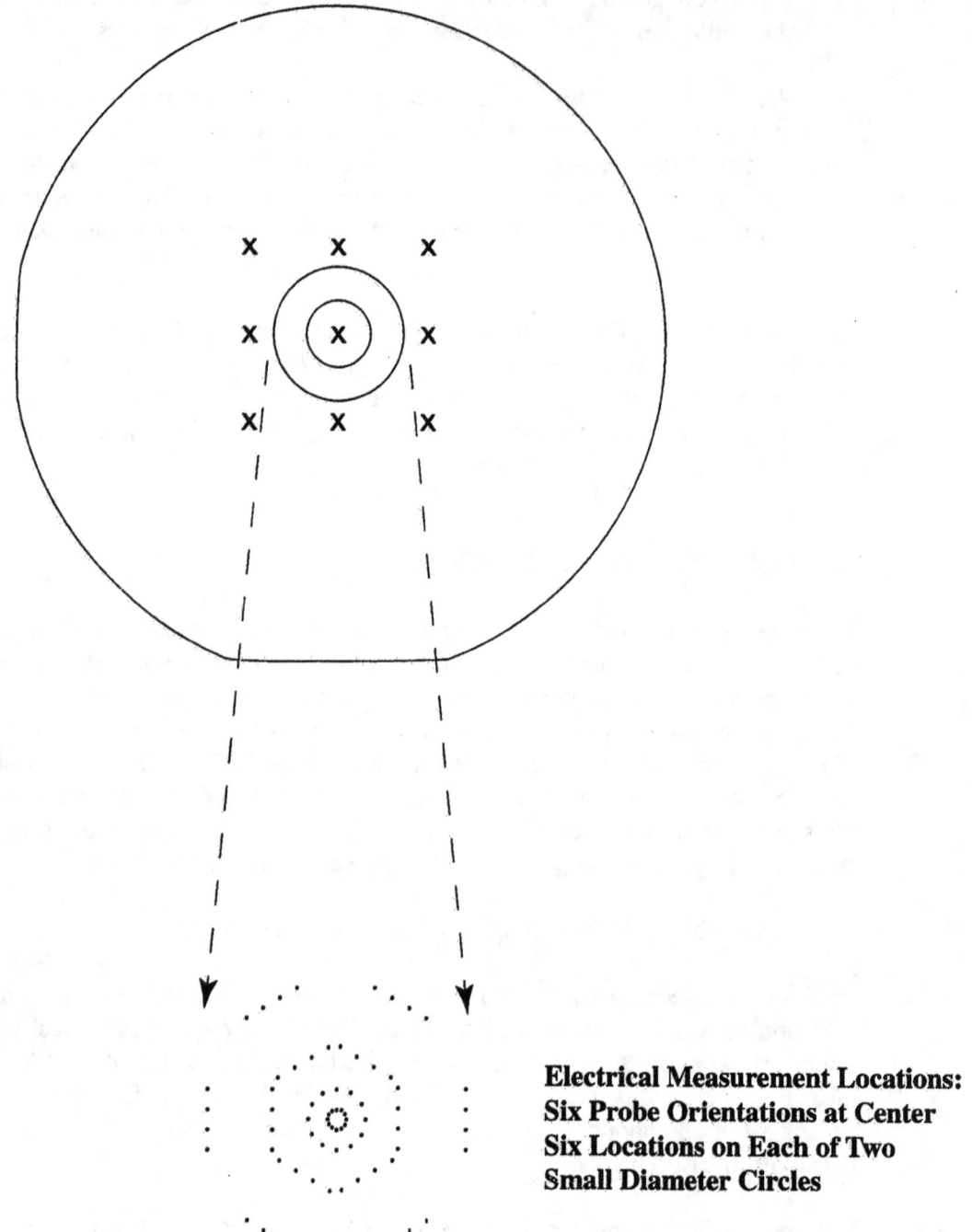

**Electrical Measurement Locations:
Six Probe Orientations at Center
Six Locations on Each of Two
Small Diameter Circles**

Figure 1. Scaled drawing of a 100 mm diameter wafer (top) showing locations of thickness measurements (x) and locations of the four-point probe measurements in the 2X magnification at the bottom.

10

variation in thickness values obtained by this instrument than those obtained by the capacitance gauge. Nevertheless, the range of thicknesses from this nine-point sampling plan is less than 0.5 μm for most wafers, and wafers are excluded from use as SRMs if there is an indicated variation of more than 1 μm among the nine sites. The average of all nine thickness values is used for conversion from sheet resistance to resistivity values on the SRM certificates. (ASTM Method F84 requires the use of only the thickness measured at the wafer center for this conversion.) The use of a nine-point average thickness reduces small errors due to local fluctuations in surface texture, is more representative of the area over which electrical measurements are taken, and improves the consistency among all wafers certified at a given SRM level. The standard deviation of these nine measurements is reported on each certificate for each wafer. Specifications for the electronic micrometer used for the thickness measurements can be found in Section 5.2.4.

2.2 Four-Probe Measurements of Sheet Resistance

Certification measurements are taken using a single four-point probe head, selected from five available (see 3.1). The specific probe used may differ from one resistivity level to another according to results of preliminary tests. All probe heads are constructed with in-line mounted tungsten-carbide probe pins, with a nominal separation of 1.59 mm between adjacent pins, with a spring-loaded force of about 1.5 N per pin and a nominal 40 μm (0.0016 in) tip radius. Eighteen sites are measured on each wafer, and wafers are allowed to equilibrate with the environment of the lab module for at least 24 h and with the temperature of the heat sink on the probe station for at least 1 min before being measured. Basic equipment requirements for all measurements follow ASTM Method F84; manufacturers' specifications for the equipment used can be found in Section 5.2.1. The measurement procedure for the first wiring configuration at each site follows ASTM F84, and that for the second configuration follows ASTM F1529 [6].

At each of the 18 sites for electrical measurement, the probe is connected first to the dc current source and DVM as in ASTM F84 (current through the outer probes and potential drop across the wafer measured with the inner probes). The current supply is set to give a specimen voltage drop between 9.95 mV and 10.05 mV for the forward current polarity at the first wafer-center measurement site. The current-supply controls remain set at this position for all remaining measurements on the wafer. The standard resistor for measurement of current value is chosen so that the voltage across the standard resistor is larger than that across the wafer. Applied current and specimen voltages are measured for both current polarities, and the average voltage-to-current ratio is calculated from these "forward" and "reverse" readings (to eliminate Seebeck voltages) [7]. Standard resistor and wafer voltages are recorded to a resolution of 0.1 μV. (More detail on the voltage measurements is given in Sec. 5.2.1.) While still in contact with the wafer, the probe head is connected to the current supply and DVM in the second wiring configuration, with the current passing between one outer probe pin and the nonadjacent interior pin, and the specimen voltages being measured with the two remaining pins. Again, forward and reverse direction current and wafer voltage values are measured, and an average voltage-to-current ratio is calculated. (See Fig. 2 for

11

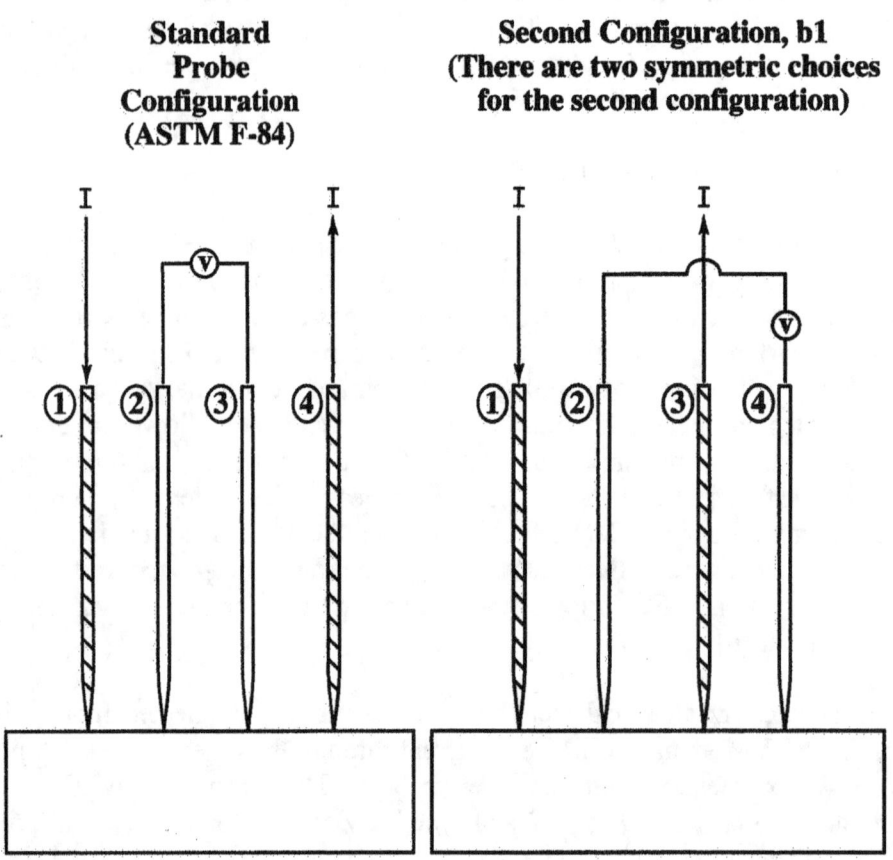

Figure 2. Schematic of probe wiring for dual-configuration measurements.

schematic of probe wiring.) For the wafers being certified, only one of the two nominally symmetric choices for this second wiring configuration is used, although both choices are used for measurement of the "control" wafers.

Using a theoretically derived relation between the voltage-to-current ratios from these two configurations, a scaling factor for lateral geometry effects is calculated [6]. This scaling factor, K_a, in eq (1) of Section 4, is multiplied by the voltage-to-current ratio from the first configuration to give a value for sheet resistance that has been corrected for wafer-edge boundary condition effects, and for variations of probe separation (at least to first order); an additional scaling factor is required if the wafer thickness is more than about 0.4 times the probe spacing (the largest ratio of wafer-thickness-to-probe-spacing for any of the SRM wafers is 0.4008). Multiplication of the sheet resistance values by wafer thickness produces values of wafer resistivity. The measurement results are corrected to 23 °C using the temperature of the heat sink at time of measurement and empirical temperature coefficients of resistivity [1].

A complete control and certification procedure is applied to a batch (approximately 125 wafers) at one of the seven resistivity levels; all data are analyzed for that batch and any necessary auxiliary measurements taken before proceeding to another resistivity level. This is to assure that any wear-induced drift, or other change that may be experienced by any of the four-point probes being used, is contained in and analyzed as part of the certification of a single batch. Two levels of control detailed in Sections 3.1 and 3.2 are used. In the first, and simpler part of certification control, a monitor-, or check-wafer, selected at random from the batch being certified, is measured at random times at least twice a day, during actual certification, to check for time-of-measurement effects due to factors other than changes in the probe. In the second part, a formal control experiment is conducted just prior to and just following the certification measurements. The entire cycle for initial control-wafer measurements, certification data for a batch of wafers, and final control-wafer measurements takes approximately 5 to 6 weeks.

2.3 Reporting of Data from 18 Measurements on Each Wafer

The 18 electrical measurement sites are distributed as follows: 1) six are located at the wafer center, with the wafer being rotated 30° between them, 2) six are spaced 60° apart around a circle of 5 mm (0.2 in) radius, and 3) six are spaced 60° apart around a circle of 10 mm (0.39 in) radius. (See Fig. 1.)

Average values of both sheet resistance and resistivity are reported for the center of the wafer, where wafer nonuniformity effects should be negligible. For measurements taken around the 5 mm and 10 mm radius circles, where additional variability due to material nonuniformity can be detected, individual site values are reported. To reduce clutter on the certificate, these individual values are given only for sheet resistance. A procedure for converting them to resistivity values follows eq (1), and is outlined on the certificate using values that are specific to each individual wafer. The data entries on the certificate are generally only

13

significant to several counts in the last digit. This digit is retained, however, to avoid additional error due to truncation.

The values reported for the two circles give the user a measure of the radial variation of resistivity for the wafer, although some azimuthal variation can also be detected on many wafers. This radial variation information is important for improving measurement transfer to instrument types having different integration volumes from that of the four-point probe used for certification. However, it is left to the user to determine how to weight the resistivities from the three regions of the wafer for the particular application of interest.

In cases where the user does not specifically need the resistance information from the 5 mm and 10 mm circles, it is strongly suggested that only the certified values from the wafer center be considered and that all user measurements be restricted to the wafer center.

3. CONTROL PROCEDURES FOR THE CERTIFICATION PROCESS

3.1 Control Procedure for Probe Effects

Immediately prior to certification of a batch of wafers and again at the end of certification, a "control" experiment is performed as follows. Each of five wafers, referred to as "control-wafers" and randomly selected from the batch to be certified, is measured for six orientations of the probe at the wafer center, using each of five probe heads in turn and the dual-configuration procedure. For the reason discussed in the next paragraph (criterion 4), both choices for the second wiring configuration are used for this test. This sequence is repeated until six rounds of measurements have been obtained on each wafer with each probe; the order of probes used and of the wafers measured is randomized for each round. Experience has shown that there is no reason to extend these measurements over a protracted period of time; this test is completed in about 7 days. The results are analyzed to give baseline values so the performance of the probe to be used for certification can be checked later if needed, to provide both short-term and longer-term estimates of measurement precision at that resistivity level, and to estimate the contribution to measurement uncertainty of the choice of measurement probe. For this latter purpose, the five available probes are assumed to represent a random sampling of all possible probes meeting reasonable operating requirements; they are not brought to like-new conditions prior to the tests. Probe heads are, however, prechecked for a number of operating characteristics, and individual pins replaced, if necessary.

After the results of the initial control experiment are analyzed, one of the probes is selected for certification measurements of all wafers in the batch. The following criteria are used when reviewing the initial control-wafer test data: 1) preference is given to probes with low average within-run standard deviations for six replicate runs on the five wafers; 2) preference is given to probes having high reproducibility of average value from the six rounds for each of the wafers; 3) preference is given to a probe that gives resistivity values in the middle of the distribution for the six-round, five-probe, five-wafer data set which should ensure minimum bias to the ensuing certification data; and 4) preference is given to probes having good consistency of measured values between the two choices for wiring the second measurement configuration. Experience has shown that most probes do not give exactly the same measurement results on bulk substrate wafers for the two choices of second configuration. The small differences that are generally seen are believed due to the inability of dual-configuration measurements on bulk silicon to completely account for variations in probe spacing. Therefore, it is important to identify, and use for certification, probes that behave according to the theory for dual-configuration measurements where the theory does not admit to a distinction between the two choices for the second measurement configuration. There is no a priori formula or weighting factor used for these preference criteria; the goal is simply to identify and use the probe that has the lowest short-term and longer-term "noise" or imprecision and the least bias in measurement results.

This control experiment is repeated upon completion of the certification measurements for a wafer batch. This repetition is used to test for a change in response of the probe used for certification (which would indicate wear or contamination during certification). This should be distinguished from possible drift that might show up for most, or all, of the probes and which would more likely be due to changes in the measurement environment or to changes in the control-wafers themselves. Small changes in the response of only the certification probe would need to be accounted for by use of an additional contribution to the uncertainty statement for the SRM value. Larger changes in the response of the certification probe, if they occur, might require the probe to be rebuilt, and the entire sequence comprising initial control experiment, probe selection, batch certification, and final control experiment to be repeated. Changes in the response of all probes, if observed, would be analyzed for consistency or randomness of behavior and appropriate components estimated for the uncertainty statement.

Data from this multi-wafer control experiment also serve to estimate short-, intermediate-, and longer-term random variations in the certification process; see Appendix 2.

3.2 Control Procedure for Day-to-Day (Environmental) Effects

Acquisition of all the certification data on a batch of about 125 wafers takes approximately 10 to 12 days. Humidity is monitored, and no wafers are measured when relative humidity readings are in excess of 50 %. To monitor for possible effects due to changes in humidity, power-line fluctuations, or similar environmental problems, one wafer from the batch, referred to as a "monitor-wafer" or "check-wafer," is measured at random times approximately twice a day for the duration of certification. This results in 20 to 30 sets of measurements on the check-wafer (six wafer-center measurement sites each); this number is well below any level that has been found to cause significant change of value due to accumulated probing damage. These check-wafer data are analyzed for possible day-to-day (or time-of-day) variations in value, either random or systematic, that need to be incorporated into the uncertainty statement. The check-wafer data can also be used to give another

15

estimate of the short-term precision of the measurement process, and may serve to corroborate wear or contamination in the certifying probe.

3.3 Control Procedure for Other Longer Term Effects and Drift of Wafer or Probe

The sets of control-wafer measurements that are taken both before and after the certification data can be used to determine whether average resistivity has increased or decreased between the two series of measurements. If they have changed by a statistically significant amount, the multiplicity of probes involved can be used to determine whether the changes are likely due to wear of the certification probe (only that probe should show significant change) or whether the same changes are detected by most or all of the probes being used. The latter condition would indicate likely changes in the control wafers themselves or in the measurement equipment. Appropriate follow-up tests would then need to be made or suitable additional terms added to the uncertainty statement.

4. EQUATIONS USED FOR CALCULATING SHEET RESISTANCE AND RESISTIVITY VALUES

The following equations are used for calculating sheet resistance and resistivity values from dual-configuration four-probe measurements.

$$R_s = \frac{V}{I} K_a \, F_T \, F(t/S) = X \, K_a \, F_T \, F(t/S) \tag{1}$$

$$\rho = \frac{V}{I} K_a \, F_T \, t \, F(t/S) = X \, K_a \, F_T \, t \, F(t/S) \tag{2}$$

where:
   R_s is the sheet resistance of the wafer, in ohms;
   ρ is the volume resistivity of the wafer, in ohm centimeters;
   (V/I) is the first-configuration (ASTM F84) voltage-to-current ratio (also called R_a), in ohms;
   t is the wafer thickness, in centimeters;
   S is the average probe separation, in centimeters;
   $F(t/S)$ is a thickness-related scaling factor (near unity for $t < 0.4$ S);
   F_T is a correction from the temperature of measurement to a reference temperature (23 °C);
   K_a is a geometric scaling factor that is calculated from electrical data in the two configurations; and
   X is a shorthand for the voltage-to-current ratio in the first configuration.

16

The equations are applied at each measurement site to the average of the voltage-to-current ratio for the forward and reverse currents.

From the theoretical development of the dual-configuration measurement, the scaling factor, K_a, is determined from a transcendental equation from reference [8], but a simplified calculation that is a highly accurate representation is given by the following quadratic equation, also from reference [8]

$$K_a = -14.696 + 25.173 \left(\frac{R_a}{R_b}\right) - 7.872 \left(\frac{R_a}{R_b}\right)^2 , \qquad (3)$$

where R_a is the voltage-to-current ratio in the first electrical configuration, and R_b is the voltage-to-current ratio in the second electrical configuration.

4.1 Rewriting the Equation to Relate to Evaluation of Uncertainty

In the ISO formulation of uncertainty, the standard uncertainty is the square-root of the sum of variances of the components evaluated by Type A procedures and of those evaluated by Type B procedures. Those components (e.g., short-, intermediate-, and longer-term measurement system imprecision) that enter through the measurement data are evaluated by statistical analysis of the actual measurements, in units of resistivity, and give a Type A standard uncertainty directly in units of resistivity. Those that enter through one of the scaling or correction factors in eq (1) or eq (2) must be multiplied by an appropriate prefactor to give a Type B standard uncertainty in the same units. The development of these prefactors is most readily done through a propagation of variance formulation for the variance of resistivity, $\sigma^2(\rho)$, in terms of the variances of the quantities in eq (2). The variance of resistivity can then be expressed as:

$$\sigma^2(\rho) = (t^2 F^2(t/S)) \, [F_T^2 \sigma^2(\chi) + \chi^2 \sigma^2(F_T)] + \left(\frac{\rho}{tF(t/S)}\right)^2 [F^2(t/S) \; \sigma^2(t) + t^2 \sigma^2(F(t/S))], \quad (4)$$

where χ is the product $X \, K_a$.

All certification and control experiment data that are supplied for statistical analysis are in units of resistivity, corrected to a temperature of 23 °C, with dimensions of ohm centimeters. The statistical variations in these data are principally manifestations of variations in the measured electrical quantities: the first term in eq (4); and to a lesser extent, variations in the temperature of measurement and the associated temperature correction: the second term in eq (4). Since each of the wafers being analyzed has a fixed assigned thickness value, there is no statistical variation due to thickness: the last two terms in eq (4). The statistical analyses

17

look at total change in resistivity from all sources and are not partitioned into variability of voltage and current or temperature correction. The results of the statistical analyses give values of uncertainty, in ohm centimeters, from which a Type A variance, in ohm centimeters squared, is calculated and then summed with the Type B variance.

All terms in eq (4) need to be considered in ISO Type B analyses of uncertainty related to measurement scale calibration errors. All terms, as written, have dimensions of ohm centimeters squared, but it is convenient to rearrange the first square-bracketed term of the equation so that it shows the same explicit dependence on ρ^2 that can be seen for the second square-bracketed term. By multiplying numerator and denominator of the first term by χ^2/F_T^2, the equation can be rewritten as:

$$\sigma^2(\rho) = \frac{\rho^2}{\chi^2 F_T^2} \left[F_T^2 \sigma^2(\chi) + \chi^2 \sigma^2 (F_T) \right] + \frac{\rho^2}{t^2 F^2(t/S)} \left[F^2(t/S) \; \sigma^2(t) + t^2 \sigma^2 (F(t/S)) \right] . \quad (5)$$

It is useful to summarize the nominal values of the various terms that appear as part of prefactors in eq (5). All such terms are sufficiently constant from wafer to wafer that use of nominal values will suffice. Nominal wafer thickness is 0.628 cm; the thickness-related scaling term $F(t/S)$ is dimensionless and is taken as unity for all wafers because of the values of t/S for the wafers being certified. The temperature correction factor, F_T, is dimensionless and is very close to unity, being no smaller than 0.985, nor larger than 1.005 for any SRM wafer. The term K_a is dimensionless and has a slightly different value for each line of data for each wafer, but the value is always close to 4.50.

In order to facilitate Type B evaluation of measurement uncertainties, it is helpful to split the preceding equation into separate variance terms that can be related to the background discussions of Type B standard uncertainty evaluations in Section 3. These terms deal with:

electrical measurements:

$$\frac{\rho^2}{\chi^2 F_T^2} \left[F_T^2 \; \sigma^2(\chi) \right] = \rho^2 \left(\frac{\sigma^2(V/I)}{(V/I)^2} + \frac{\sigma^2(K_a)}{K_a^2} \right) , \quad (5a)$$

temperature measurements:

$$\frac{\rho^2}{\chi^2 F_T^2} \left[\chi^2 \; \sigma^2(F_T) \right] = \frac{\rho^2 \; \sigma^2(F_T)}{F_T^2} , \quad (5b)$$

18

and thickness measurements:

$$\frac{\rho^2}{t^2 \ F^2(t/S)} \ [F^2(t/S) \ \sigma^2(t) \ + \ t^2 \ \sigma^2 \ (F(t/S))] \ = \ \rho^2 \left(\frac{\sigma^2(t)}{t^2} \ + \ \frac{\sigma^2(F(t/S))}{F^2(t/S)} \right). \qquad (5c)$$

Thus, following this rearrangement, each of the contributions reduces to the relative variance of a variable times the square of the resistivity.

5. SOURCES OF MEASUREMENT UNCERTAINTY — DETAILED DISCUSSION

5.1 Type A Evaluations of Components of Uncertainty

The contributions to uncertainty from sources discussed in this section are evaluated solely from certification and control experiment data taken at the time of certification for each of the resistivity levels. A variance is calculated for each of the Type A contributions. These variances are then combined in a root-sum-of-squares fashion to give a standard deviation from the combination of effects; this standard deviation is the Type A standard uncertainty. Data from SRM 2547, at 200 Ω·cm, are used in Appendix 2 to illustrate the analysis procedures used. Abbreviated summaries from SRMs 2541, 2542, 2545, and 2546, which follow the same procedures, are given in Appendices 3 through 6 (some of these latter appendices also contain analysis details of a specific additional term which was not pertinent to the data analyzed in Appendix 2). The statistical reports in the appendices state the standard uncertainties for the resistivities at the wafer-center and for the 5 mm and 10 mm measurement circles. In Section 7, those values from Appendices 2 through 6 are summarized, the variances from Type A and Type B analyses are tabulated, and the combined variances, combined standard uncertainties, and expanded uncertainties are given for both sheet resistance and resistivity for each of the SRMs.

5.1.1 Short-term precision; repeatability
There is expected to be negligible effect from wafer nonuniformity on the six measurements at the wafer center; ideally, these measurements would all have the same value. The standard deviation of the six values is a measure of the repeatability, or short-term precision, under tightly controlled conditions. The repeatability is evaluated from data taken over periods so short that there should be no changes in measurement environment, or wear or damage effects on the wafers or the probe. The variability among the data being analyzed is a combination of two effects, both of which cause fluctuations in the voltage-to-current ratios, and as a result, in the calculated K_a scaling factor that is based on those ratios. (See eq (1).) The first of these effects is the scatter in the electrical data due to pure electrical or electronic sources such as variations in probe contact quality, power supply noise, or DVM noise; the second is scatter in electrical data due to small fluctuations in probe separation, from one site to the

19

next, that is not fully corrected for by use of the dual-configuration technique. These two effects are the primary mechanisms causing short-term data scatter; they cannot be separated functionally, and there is no need for doing so. They are accounted for in calculations of short-term standard deviation of resistivity. Typical values for the standard deviation of a set of six measurements at the center of a wafer have been found to range from 0.03 % to about 0.30 % for single-configuration data and about 0.02 % to 0.12 % for dual-configuration data. The actual values for standard deviation depend somewhat on the probe used and on the wafer resistivity level. One of the causes of the spread in the observed values is the small sample size (six measurements in the NIST certification procedure) for calculating the standard deviation. The short-term precision for the certification process at each resistivity level is estimated from a pooling of variances of the wafer-center data from the wafers being certified and similar data from the wafers in both types of control experiments. There are typically 1000 or more degrees of freedom to this pooled estimate, depending on the number of wafers in the batch being certified.

5.1.2 Intermediate and longer term precision; reproducibility of wafer-center average value

Assuming there is no significant change in the probe used for certification measurements and no change in the resistivity of any of the wafers due to the probing process, it should be possible to remeasure any of the wafers and obtain average values that fall within limits based on the short-term precision value. In fact, this generally is not found. The small excess variation is believed due to changes in the measurement environment, such as power-line variations and changes in the radiated noise in the laboratory environment, humidity changes, etc., that are not readily identified over the short time spans used to measure individual wafers. Data from the replicate measurements on the check-wafer and also from the initial and final control experiment wafers are analyzed for a day-to-day (run-to-run) random variation in the response of the certification probe that is in excess of the pooled short-term standard deviation. In addition, comparisons of preliminary and final control experiment data for each of the probes on each of the control wafers are used to estimate any additional longer-term variations that are characteristic of the entire measurement system and changes in the environment, not just of the certification probe or the check-wafer. Such contributions to uncertainty are termed "long-term variations" in the statistical analysis reports. There are typically 50 degrees of freedom in the determination of the day-to-day variability in the analysis of the control-wafer data and 20 or more degrees of freedom in such a determination from the check-wafer data. There are 5 degrees of freedom for the calculation of long-term variability in the comparison of initial and final control experiment data. The same sets of data are also analyzed for possible systematic data trends in the measurement process or specimens and corrections terms applied or additional uncertainty components evaluated, as necessary. Such a systematic trend was identified for the 200 Ω·cm wafers. It is discussed separately in Section 6, and the analysis of a resulting asymmetric modification of the uncertainty interval is given in Appendix 2.

5.1.3 Uncertainty due to the selection of a particular probe

It has been found, based on the analysis of many experiments, that resistivity measurement values obtained by four-point probe on bulk wafers have a small dependence on the probe being used. Experience at NIST shows this to be the largest residual error when ASTM Method F84 is used for measurement; measuring the geometric separation of probe impressions made on a polished wafer, as required by ASTM F84, does not adequately describe their functional electrical separation. This dependence is significantly reduced, but not eliminated, by use of the dual-configuration procedure. This may be thought of as an issue of the accuracy of the basic model of dual-configuration four-probe measurements applied to real probes having finite size contact areas and contacts that are not purely ohmic, but affected by metal-semiconductor interface effects. The result is a probe-dependent bias in the measured wafer resistance value that might normally be considered a systematic effect, the value of which could be evaluated, or estimated for any given probe. Because there is no model of the physics that causes the offset for a given probe, an estimate of the probable distribution of probe offset values cannot be done on a theoretical basis. A numerical evaluation of such a distribution could be done if given a sufficiently large number of probes, and the bias of a given probe could then be determined using the many-probe average as a point of reference. However, there are only five probe heads available for use in the certification procedure, thus making it impossible to obtain data from a sufficient variety of probe heads to generate a distribution of probe-dependence values.

Instead, the five available probe heads are treated as a random sample from the universe of probe heads, and sufficient replication data are taken with each probe head during the initial and final control experiments (Sec. 1.4) that a statistical estimate can be made for a variance term due to probes as a variable. Thus, while the choice-of-probe effect is most simply conceptualized as a systematic error, it is actually evaluated from statistical analysis of these replicate measurements as a Type A contributor to the standard uncertainty of certification. The initial and final control experiments incorporate data from both choices for wiring the second probe configuration, while the certification measurements use only one of those two choices. The initial and final control experiments are also analyzed for possible contribution to certification uncertainty due to small differences between the two choices for second configuration wiring.

5.2 Type B Evaluations of Components of Uncertainty

No corrections were applied to the SRM certification measurements for possible errors in voltage, current, or thickness values. However, a correction was applied for the difference between the temperature scale of the thermistor used to monitor measurement temperature and that of a precision mercury bulb thermometer which is the customary reference to a NIST-traceable temperature scale following the procedure of ASTM F84.

In this section, with one exception, a single value is calculated for uncertainty in electrical and thickness scales which is applicable to all resistivity levels. That exception is at 0.01 $\Omega \cdot cm$, for which the value related to electrical measurements is almost twice as large as that for the worst case from any of the higher resistivity levels. A separate value is given for 0.01 $\Omega \cdot$cm. For the temperature correction term, it is necessary to calculate a separate value for each resistivity level.

In the remainder of Section 5.2, individual effects are considered significant, and are retained, if they are at least 0.01 % (one part in ten thousand) of the measured value. Values smaller than that are considered negligible.

5.2.1 Discussion of components related to electrical measurements

Measurement of Specimen Current — Four separate precision-current supplies are available, each calibrated and tested annually for ripple and noise. Measurement accuracy does not rely on this calibration, however. Instead, the measurement current is fed through a precision standard resistor in series with the wafer, and the voltage drop across the resistor is measured with the same 6-1/2 digit DVM (Hewlett-Packard model 3456) used for the silicon wafer measurements. Voltage measurements are taken with a resolution of 0.1 μV. Five precision resistors from 0.01 Ω to 1000 Ω are available. Each is calibrated periodically at NIST. The resistors have calibration uncertainties of 3 $\mu\Omega/\Omega$ to 5 $\mu\Omega/\Omega$. There is no meaningful change of value of these resistors due to temperature variations for the temperature excursions encountered in the lab. Standard resistor and wafer voltages are measured on the same range setting of the DVM. In typical practice, a standard resistor is selected for use so that it gives a voltage drop that is a factor of 1 to 10 times that of the specimen being measured; e.g., a 10 Ω standard resistor is used for the measurement of a 1 $\Omega \cdot$cm wafer. Voltages measured across the standard resistor are typically 25 mV, generally stable to 1 μV and read to 0.1 μV. One of the two available solid-state power supplies is preferred for measurement because of the convenience of six-digit current selection; however, the regulation specifications for these current supplies (as a percent of full-scale) become marginal for the low currents used when measuring 100 $\Omega \cdot$cm and 200 $\Omega \cdot$cm SRMs, and it has been found preferable to switch to a vacuum-tube supply to maximize measurement current stability for these resistivities. Specifications for the current supplies and for the digital voltmeter are given in Table 1.

Measurement of Specimen Voltages — ASTM Method F84 requires that the measurement current be set to give a specimen voltage drop, between the two inner probes, of 10 mV to 20 mV. NIST measurements for SRMs 1521 to 1523 were taken in the restricted range of 10 mV to 12 mV. For the 100 mm SRMs, 2541 to 2547, reported here, measurements are taken in the still more restrictive range of 9.95 mV to 10.05 mV. (See Sec. 2.2.) (With a 1.59 mm probe point separation, this gives a maximum field of less than 7 mV/mm across the wafer.) Once the current is adjusted to give a specimen voltage in this range for the ASTM wiring configuration of the very first measurement at the wafer center, the power supply is left at this setting for all other measurements on that wafer. This specimen voltage range results in an acceptable number of digits of measurement resolution with minimal risk of Joule heating or minority carrier injection. The only exception to this procedure occurs for wafers with low resistivity (below about 0.05 $\Omega \cdot$cm for a nominal 625 μm thickness) where use of a current supply having a typical 100 mA maximum output will result in a maximum obtainable specimen voltage that is below the range stated above. For the lowest resistivity

SRM, 0.01 Ω·cm, the specimen voltage at 100 mA is about 3.1 mV; this causes a somewhat larger relative uncertainty in the scale of the electrical measurements at this SRM level.

Typical stability of wafer voltage readings, as seen from the DVM display, ranges from ±1 μV to ±3 μV (depending upon resistivity, probe, and environmental conditions). In practice, after setting the switches for each desired voltage to be measured, the operator verifies that there is no drift in the DVM display for that setting by observing five to ten readings, and then causes the next DVM reading to be stored in the computer with the expectation that the scatter noted above represents a random error in the stored value.

Although the single DVM reading that is stored for each voltage or current measurement can be said to be in error as long as there is any scatter in the DVM displays observed by the operator, it is not necessary to do a first-principles propagation of error based on typical voltage scatter and eq (5a) in order to determine the random uncertainty in the voltage-to-current ratio. The standard deviation of a set of measurements taken in a fixed region of the wafer (e.g., the wafer center where material nonuniformity effects are negligible) encompasses the uncertainty due to digital voltmeter noise just described, as well as that due to variations in probe separation and probe contact quality. Thus, these sources of error are part of the short-term Type A uncertainty of measurement discussed in Section 5.1.1. It is not necessary to do any other analysis for these factors. Accuracy, or systematic error, of the digital voltmeter is limited by the 24 count, or 2.4 μV specification. However, relative accuracy of the ratio measurement is better than 2.4 μV and is essentially controlled by the accuracy of the standard resistor values. The effect of digital voltmeter accuracy on measurement uncertainty is given in Section 5.2.2.

General Integrity of the Electronic Instrumentation — This is basically a problem of elimination/rejection of noise, whether from electronic or thermal sources. When the current supplies are sent for calibration, they are also checked to verify that they are within the manufacturers' specifications for ripple and noise; see Table 1. The primary switch-matrix in the instrumentation utilizes heavy copper contact posts and twin seven-wiper blade construction designed to be thermal-voltage free. The common-mode and normal-mode noise rejection specifications for the DVM are stated for the case of a 1000 Ω measurement load; this value is exceeded, however, for all SRMs above 1 Ω·cm. To test the effectiveness of noise rejection, as well as possible leakage currents, analog boxes with very large series resistors (that represent probe contact resistance, see ASTM F84) are measured with, and without, the series resistors in the circuit. This is done as a part of the preparation for certification of each SRM level. Worst-case experience shows that analog boxes simulating 10 000 Ω·cm silicon experience a measurement difference (error) of about 0.20 % between these two setups. This decreases to about 0.02 % when simulating 1000 Ω·cm silicon and is negligible for the simulation of 200 Ω·cm and lower resistivity silicon.

Table 1. Manufacturers' Specifications for the Current Supplies and DVM Used for Certification

ELECTRONIC MEASUREMENTS Inc. Model C612 Constant-Current Supply*

OUTPUT RANGES:	1 µA, 2.2 µA, 5 µA, multiplier x1, x10, x100 etc. to 100 mA max. (0 to 100 % vernier each range)
STABILITY:	0.3 % of range setting (fixed line, load, and temp.)
CURRENT REGULATION:	0.1 % for 100 V step in compliance voltage
RIPPLE and NOISE:	0.04 % rms of range setting + 0.5 µA (negative ground) 0.04 % rms of range setting + 0.1 µA (positive ground) (floating output is used for certification)
OUTPUT IMPEDANCE:	30 000 MΩ @ 1 µA to 500 kΩ @ 100 mA

*This current supply is operated at 50 %, or greater, of range setting.

ELECTRONIC DEVELOPMENT CORPORATION Model CR103 Constant-Current Supply

OUTPUT RANGES:	10 mA and 100 mA full scale; 6 digit setability
STABILITY (non-additive):	1 h 0.001 % of range 8 h 0.005 % " 1 Yr. 0.01 % "
RIPPLE and NOISE:	(0.1 Hz to 100 kHz) <0.5 µA
OUTPUT CONDUCTANCE:	0.1 µS
TEMPERATURE COEFFICIENT:	0.0005 %/K

Table 1. (cont'd.)

HEWLETT-PACKARD #3456 DVM
(All values are stated for the 100 mV range)

RESOLUTION (Least Count):   0.1 µV

INPUT IMPEDANCE: $>10^{10}\ \Omega$

MEASUREMENT ACCURACY: For auto-zero on, filter off and ≥10 power cycle cycles):
    24 h @ (23 ± 1) °C: ±(0.0022 % rdg. + 24 counts)
    90 day @ (23 ± 5) °C: ±(0.0034 % rdg. + 24 counts)

TEMPERATURE COEFFICIENT: ±(0.0002 % rdg. + 0.2 counts/°C)

NOISE REJECTION: Normal mode, ac: 60 dB
    (1 kΩ max. Unbalance in low)
    Common mode, ac: 150 dB
    Common mode, dc: 140 dB

5.2.2 Evaluation of uncertainty in electrical measurement scale

Electrical measurement scale contributions to the variance of resistivity value are found from examining the right-hand side of eq (5a)

$$\rho^2 \left[\frac{\sigma^2(V/I)^2}{(V/I)^2} + \frac{\sigma^2(K_a)}{(K_a)^2} \right]. \tag{6}$$

Ignoring temporarily the term in K_a, and replacing the current, I, with the ratio of standard resistor voltage to standard resistor value, V_s/R_s, in the first term, results in

$$\rho^2 \left[\frac{\sigma^2(VR_s/V_s)}{(VR_s/V_s)^2} \right] = \rho^2 \left[\frac{\sigma^2(V/V_s)}{(V/V_s)^2} + \frac{\sigma^2(R_s)}{R_s^2} \right]. \tag{7}$$

Rather than expanding the term in (V/V_s) to get separate terms in $\sigma^2(V)$ and $\sigma^2(V_s)$, it is preferable to look at the way in which electrical measurement error affects the ratio, V/V_s, as a whole. It is assumed that the 2.4 μV error (due to voltmeter accuracy limit statement) affects the measurements of V and V_s equally (both voltages are measured on the same meter, and in quick succession). Then the worst-case error in their ratio occurs when V_s is the largest multiple of V. It can be seen from Table 2 that this occurs when V_s approximately equals $3 \times V$.

For the resistivities above 0.01 Ω·cm, the wafer voltage-drop is 10 mV, the standard resistor voltage-drop is 30 mV, and the worst-case ratio V/V_s, with no error in voltage values, is 0.333 333 3. A 2.4 μV error in both V and V_s for these wafers causes a change in the ratio to 0.333 386 7. The difference of the two ratios is 0.000 053 4 and will be taken as a limit of error in the voltage ratios due to DVM least-count error. Squaring this value, and dividing by 3 (assuming a rectangular error distribution) gives a variance of 9.50×10^{-10}. The denominator, $(V/V_s)^2$, equals 0.111, so the contribution to variance from the first term above is: $(9.50 \times 10^{-10}/0.111)\, \rho^2$, or $8.56 \times 10^{-9}\, \rho^2$.

At 0.01 Ω·cm, because of smaller measurement voltage levels, the contribution to uncertainty from electrical measurements is actually larger than the worst-case value for the SRMs above 0.01 Ω·cm. For this SRM level, the ratio without voltage measurement error, is 3.1 mV/10 mV, or 0.310 000; and with a 2.4 μV error, it is 0.310 166. The resulting error in the V/V_s ratio is 0.000 166. Squaring this, and dividing by 3, as above, gives 9.18×10^{-9}. The denominator, $(V/V_s)^2$, at 0.01 Ω·cm, is 0.096. The resulting contribution to variance of resistivity, at 0.01 Ω·cm, is $9.56 \times 10^{-8}\, \rho^2$.

The second term in eq (7),

$$\frac{\rho^2\ \sigma^2(R_s)}{R_s^2},$$

can be shown to be negligible. The calibration uncertainty of all standard resistors used for the SRMs is $<5 \times 10^{-6}$ times the value of the resistor. Assuming a rectangular distribution for standard resistor calibration error, $\sigma^2(R_s)/(R_s)^2 = (2.5 \times 10^{-11}/3) = 8.3 \times 10^{-12}$. The contribution to variance related to standard resistor calibration error is $8.3 \times 10^{-12}\, \rho^2$ and is negligible. Likewise, possible contributions due to drift, or to temperature dependence of standard resistor values are negligible compared to the one part in ten-thousand criterion noted above.

Table 2. Standard Resistor Values, and Typical Measurement Voltages
for Each of the SRM Levels

Nominal SRM Value ($\Omega \cdot$cm)	Standard Resistor (Ω)	SRM Wafer Voltage, V (mV)	Std. Res. Voltage, V_s (mV)
0.01	0.1	3.1	10
0.1	1	10	25
1	10	10	25
10	100	10	25
25	100	10	11.5
100	1000	10	30
200	1000	10	14

The other contribution to uncertainty due to electrical measurement scale error comes from the second term in eq (5a)

$$\rho^2 \left[\frac{\sigma^2(K_a)}{K_a^2} \right].$$

K_a has the following characteristics. It is the solution to a transcendental equation based on two configurations of electrical data taken at each measurement site. The solution has been approximated by a quadratic equation in the argument R_a/R_b, where R_a is the ratio of V/I in the first (ASTM) wiring configurations and X_b is the V/I ratio in one of the two choices for the second configuration. Specifically, the quadratic equation is

$$K_a = -14.696 + 25.173 \left(\frac{R_a}{R_b} \right) - 7.872 \left(\frac{R_a}{R_b} \right)^2.$$

The accuracy of the fit over the range $1.20 < R_a/R_b < 1.32$ is reported to be better than 0.05 % [9]. For the wafer diameter, measurement locations, and probe size used in this SRM certification, the ratio, R_a/R_b, is approximately 1.255. There are small variations, from about 1.25 to 1.26, which encompass both the effects of electrical measurement noise and small fluctuations in the separation of adjacent pairs of probe pins from one measurement position to the next. A ratio of R_a/R_b of 1.255 results in a K_a value of about 4.50. Over this restricted range, the accuracy of fit of the quadratic, is actually about 0.01 %.

27

There are two independent considerations in evaluating $\sigma^2(K_a)$. The first is the relative inaccuracy, 0.01 %, of the quadratic representation of the transcendental equation. With the assumption of a uniform probability distribution, it results in a contribution to the variance of $[\{(0.000\,1\,K_a)^2/3\}/K_a^2] \times \rho^2$, or $3.33 \times 10^{-9}\,\rho^2$.

The second is the error in K_a that would occur because of an error in measured voltages. For a nominal value of $R_d/R_b = 1.255$, and any of the SRMs above 0.01 Ω·cm, a voltage measurement error of 2.4 μV would cause an error in R_d/R_b of no more than 0.000 07. This causes a change (error) in K_a of about 0.000 38. Again assuming a rectangular distribution of error, this means that the voltage error contribution to variance is $[\{(0.000\,38)^2/3\}/(4.50)^2] \times \rho^2$ or about $2.39 \times 10^{-9}\,\rho^2$. For the 0.01 Ω·cm SRM, and under the same assumptions, a voltage error of 2.4 μV causes an error in the ratio, R_d/R_b, of 0.000 24. This, in turn, results in an error in K_a of 0.001 29 and a contribution to the variance of ρ^2 at 0.01 Ω·cm of $[\{(0.001\,29)^2/3\}/(4.50)^2] \times \rho^2$, or about $2.74 \times 10^{-8}\,\rho^2$.

Adding these terms to that for possible error due to the quadratic representation of the transcendental equation, the variance in ρ^2 due to possible error in the factor, K_a, is $3.07 \times 10^{-8}\,\rho^2$ at 0.01 Ω·cm, and is $5.72 \times 10^{-9}\,\rho^2$ for SRMs above 0.01 Ω·cm.

No specific additional systematic error terms due to instrumentation integrity have been identified in the resistivity range of these SRMs other than the 0.02 % offset that has been seen with the 1000 Ω analog box. Noise, due to poor contact quality, radiated signal pickup, or other sources, may be present. It is believed to contribute scatter, in the low microvolt level, to the data, and show up as a component of the standard deviation of the data. It is possible, but has not proven necessary, to integrate measurements on the DVM for 100 power-line cycles, instead of the customary 10 cycles, to suppress the effects of ac pickup.

Therefore, the total contribution to variance of resistivity due to electrical measurement considerations discussed above is $1.263 \times 10^{-7}\,\rho^2$ at 0.01 Ω·cm and $1.428 \times 10^{-8}\,\rho^2$ at all higher resistivities.

5.2.3 Evaluation of uncertainty components related to temperature measurements
The variance of resistivity value due to temperature measurement errors arises as follows: During resistivity measurement, each wafer is placed on a copper block which is both massive, to maintain temperature stability, and made of a good thermal conductor, to enhance the speed of equilibration of temperature between the surface where the wafer is located and the block's interior where the thermistor temperature sensor is located. A thin mica film provides electrical insulation between the wafer and the copper block. The measured temperature (maintained in the range 22 °C to 24 °C for all SRM wafer measurements and observed to be stable to 0.1 °C, or better, for any given SRM wafer) is used in conjunction with an empirically evaluated temperature coefficient of resistivity for silicon to correct the measured resistivity to the standard value of 23 °C. The temperature coefficient of resistivity for silicon, which is a function of both resistivity and conductivity type, was evaluated at NBS in the mid-1960's. This temperature coefficient is used internationally and is part of a

standard measurement procedure (ASTM F84) for silicon resistivity near room temperature. It is expected that all users of these SRMs for application to silicon technology will use the same temperature coefficients for interpretation of their "unknown" or "test" wafers. No evaluation of uncertainty of the coefficient itself is made here.

The thermistor was calibrated against a precision mercury bulb thermometer over the range 15 °C to 35 °C. The mercury bulb thermometer itself was calibrated by NIST with a stated uncertainty of ±0.03 °C, or better. Thermistor resolution is better than 0.01 °C. Transfer uncertainty between glass bulb and thermistor is estimated to be no worse than 0.02 °C; a value of 0.02 °C will be used. The largest potential error is that the copper block temperature may not be the same as that of the wafer. This could be due to warm or cool air currents from the room ventilation system affecting the wafer and block exterior. Tests of consistency of resistivity measurement with controlled temperature increase and decrease indicate that potential error between sensor and wafer is less than ±0.08 °C. The calibrations of the glass bulb thermometer and that of the thermistor are added to give a worst-case temperature calibration error of ±0.05 °C. This is added linearly to the possible wafer-sensor offset of 0.08 °C to give a worst case total temperature error of 0.13 °C.

Because all possible temperature errors were added linearly to calculate worst-case error, above, it is overly conservative to assume a uniform distribution of error to calculate a variance, and a triangular distribution for the temperature error is assumed instead. Thus, the variance of the distribution of possible temperature error is $(0.13 \ °C)^2/6 = 0.002 \ 82 \ (°C)^2$.

To minimize possible temperature error in practice, wafers are kept in the vicinity of the measurement station for at least 24 h prior to measurement, and have at least 1 min to stabilize on the copper block before taking measurements. Possible errors in resistivity values due to temperature enter through the term from the right-hand side of eq (5b)

$$ \rho^2 \ \frac{\sigma^2(F_T)}{F_T^2} \ , $$

where the temperature correction of resistivity, F_T, has the form,

$$ F_T = 1 - C_T (T - 23 \ °C) \ , $$

where C_T is the temperature coefficient of resistivity, in degree Celsius^{-1}, and T is the temperature at which measurements are made, in degree Celsius.

The variance in F_T is really the variance in temperature (given above) times the square of the temperature coefficient, $(C_T)^2$. Since the coefficient, C_T, varies noticeably as a function of

29

resistivity value, Table 3 summarizes the values of the temperature coefficient used in the calculation of uncertainty.

Table 3. Temperature Coefficients of Resistivity of Silicon
for the Nominal Values of the SRMs[*]

Nom. Res. ($\Omega \cdot$cm)	0.01	0.1	1	10	25	100	200
Temp. Coeff. ($^\circ$C)$^{-1}$	0.0031	0.0041	0.0071	0.0082	0.0083	0.0083	0.0083

*Exact values are given on the certificate for each SRM wafer.

The variance of resistivity value due to temperature error is $0.002\,82\,(C_T)^2\,\rho^2$. Because of the difference in the values of C_T for the various SRM levels, the variance in resistivity value due to temperature error is given in Table 4.

Table 4. Variance in Resistivity Value Due to Temperature Error

SRM Resistivity $\Omega \cdot$cm	$\sigma^2(F_T)$	Contribution to Variance of Resistivity
0.01	2.71×10^{-8}	$2.71 \times 10^{-8}\,\rho^2$
0.1	4.51×10^{-8}	$4.51 \times 10^{-8}\,\rho^2$
1	1.42×10^{-7}	$1.42 \times 10^{-7}\,\rho^2$
10	1.90×10^{-7}	$1.90 \times 10^{-7}\,\rho^2$
25	1.94×10^{-7}	$1.94 \times 10^{-7}\,\rho^2$
100	1.94×10^{-7}	$1.94 \times 10^{-7}\,\rho^2$
200	1.94×10^{-7}	$1.94 \times 10^{-7}\,\rho^2$

5.2.4 Evaluation of the uncertainty components related to geometry measurements
In single configuration (ASTM F84) measurements by four-point probe, it is necessary to measure accurately the wafer diameter, the wafer thickness, the average separation between the probe pins, and variability thereof, in order to calculate geometry-related scaling factors that convert measured voltage/current ratios to sheet resistance and resistivity values. In dual-configuration measurements, only the measurement of wafer thickness and the average probe separation (for thicker wafers) enters into the calculation of sheet resistance and

resistivity. The following discussion deals with errors in geometry measurements as they relate to possible uncertainties in the certification values.

Comments on Nonideality of a Lapped Surface — A lapped surface texture is used to optimize electrical stability of the SRMs and to improve contact quality between the probe and wafer. The wafer thickness, in centimeters, is used to multiply sheet resistance values to convert them to resistivity values. Fractional errors in thickness values are reflected 1:1 as fractional errors in calculated resistivity values. The lapped wafer surface has a peak-and-valley texture that is related to, but generally smaller in size than, the abrasive used to do the lapping. Even though the lapping process used to prepare the SRM wafers is known to give total (macroscopic) thickness uniformity better than obtainable on as-cut or polished wafers, the existence of the surface texture precludes there being a unique thickness value at any location on the wafer. (The 100 mm SRM wafers for SRMs 2541 to 2547 were lapped with a simultaneous two-side lapping process. An abrasive grit size of about 12 μm was used for the four lowest resistivities and a 7 μm grit size for the three highest resistivities. The earlier 50.8 mm (2 in) diameter NBS silicon resistivity SRMs utilized a one-side-at-a-time process and a 5 μm abrasive. As a result, the 100 mm wafers have much improved macroscopic thickness uniformity, but a somewhat coarser surface texture compared with earlier SRMs.)

Measured thickness values are somewhat dependent on the method of measurement. Electromechanical-, capacitive-, acoustic-, or air-gauges are not expected to respond the same to the hills and valleys of a textured surface or to average over the same surface area. A mechanical method that measures front-surface-to-back-surface peak-to-peak thickness is the most idealized conceptually when dealing with these circumstances, and was used for thickness measurements of the SRM wafers. However, the peak heights on a lapped surface are somewhat variable on both wafer faces (resulting in small local fluctuations in peak-to-peak thickness and some sensitivity to the location where the thickness measurements are made). Figure 3 attempts to illustrate the situation of defining and measuring thickness on a textured surface using an electromechanical gauge.

Calibration and Control of the Electronic-Micrometer — Wafer thicknesses of the SRMs were measured with an electronic-micrometer having a resolution of 0.05 μm and a short-term repeatability of about 0.1 μm. The instrument's specifications state that its accuracy is ±0.1 μm if the ambient temperature is kept at 20 °C ± 1 °C. The requirement of a temperature of 20 °C is based on the temperature at which the instrument was calibrated by the manufacturer. While the laboratory at NIST in which the instrument is used maintains the required 1 °C temperature stability, the nominal working temperature is typically 23 °C. To maintain the calibration accuracy of the micrometer, standard practice is to calibrate, and to recheck, the instrument a number of times a day against precision gauge blocks traceable to NIST and having thicknesses that are comparable to the SRM wafers. The gauge readout was reset, as necessary, to match the gauge block value. Thus, the thickness measurement for the SRMs was a process of transfer of thickness value from a gauge block through the thickness

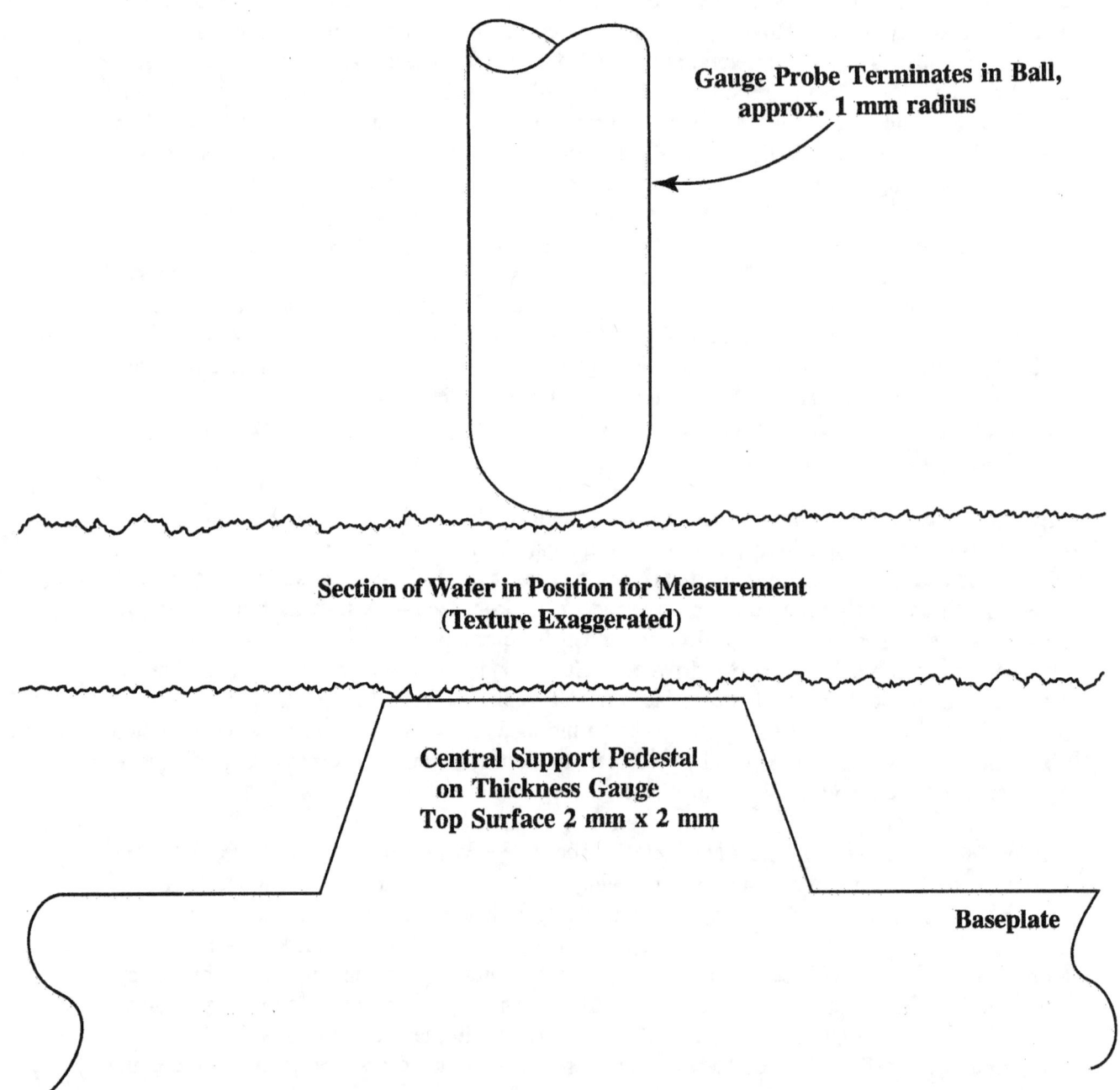

Gauge Probe Terminates in Ball, approx. 1 mm radius

Section of Wafer in Position for Measurement (Texture Exaggerated)

Central Support Pedestal on Thickness Gauge Top Surface 2 mm x 2 mm

Baseplate

Figure 3. Conceptual drawing of wafer with two textured surfaces during thickness measurement by electromechanical gauge.

gauge to the wafer. Several error components can be identified that will affect the accuracy of this transfer. The thickness gauge specifications are given in Table 5.

[**Note**: These resistivity SRMs are not intended to serve as thickness calibration standards, and that it goes beyond the scope of this work to be able to relate the performances of electromechanical-, capacitive-, acoustic-, air-gauge, and other thickness methodologies on lapped surface wafers.]

Table 5. Specifications for Haidenhain Certo 60 Thickness Measurement Instrument

Measurement Resolution	0.05 μm
Measurement Accuracy	±0.1 μm
(At an Operating Temp of 19 °C to 21 °C)	
Wafer Backside-Reference Pedestal	2 mm x 2 mm
Probe Tip Radius	1 mm
Probe Working Force	1 N

5.2.5 Evaluation of uncertainty due to thickness measurement scale

Possible errors in the thickness measurement scale contribute to uncertainty of resistivity directly through the first term in eq (5c),

$$\rho^2 \; \frac{\sigma(t)^2}{t^2} \; .$$

Based on the average SRM wafer thickness of 0.0628 cm, the denominator has a value of 0.003 94 cm^2.

Two error mechanisms contribute to a Type B estimate of variance of thickness values. The first relates to the calibration of the thickness measurement tool with precision gauge blocks. Three blocks with thicknesses of 0.024 in, 0.025 in, and 0.026 in (0.060 96 cm, 0.063 50 cm, and 0.066 04 cm), i.e., just spanning all expected values of wafer thickness, and having NIST-traceable thicknesses known to better than 0.000 004 in (0.000 01 cm) are used. In the tool calibration procedure, the tool is adjusted to read the known thickness of the 0.025 in (0.06350 cm) block and required to read the other two within 0.15 μm (0.000 015 cm) of their stated calibration values. This is 50 % larger than the uncertainty of individual gauge block calibration values. The value 0.000 015 cm is taken as the half-width of the rectangular

33

distribution of possible error assignable to the calibration of the thickness measurement tool. As a result, there is a contribution to variance of resistivity of $1.90 \times 10^{-8}\ \rho^2$ from possible tool calibration error.

The second error mechanism relates to the transfer of the thickness measurement scale to the SRM silicon wafers. Various tests of consistency of wafer thickness values suggests that a rectangular distribution with a 0.1 μm half-width should be sufficient to account for the thickness transfer error term. This results in a contribution to variance of resistivity of $8.37 \times 10^{-9}\ \rho^2$. Combining these two terms gives a variance of resistivity value directly due to variance of thickness of $2.74 \times 10^{-8}\ \rho^2$.

5.2.6 Evaluation of uncertainty due to thickness/probe separation scaling factor

A scaling factor, $F(t/S)$, is used to correct the calculated sheet resistance values for layers of finite thickness (greater than about 0.4 times the average probe spacing). Error in either the wafer thickness or in average probe separation value contributes to the variance of sheet resistance or resistivity through the second term in eq (5c),

$$\rho^2\ \frac{\sigma^2\ (F(t/S))}{F^2(t/S)}\ ,$$

where the denominator is effectively unity.

The scaling factor, $F(t/S)$, for dual-configuration measurements is similar to that, $F(w/S)$, for single-configuration measurements in that they both asymptotically approach unity for values of w/S just below 0.4. These scaling factors are virtually identical for values of the ratio, w/S, below about 0.45, but diverge noticeably in value for wafer thicknesses that are a large fraction, or a multiple, of the probe separation.

ASTM F84 recommends the simplification that this factor be set to unity when the ratio of wafer thickness to average probe separation is 0.4 or less. For all larger values of the ratio, the scaling factor is then computed from summation of a specified series and takes on values decreasing from unity as the ratio increases above 0.4. The ratio, 0.4, exactly corresponds to a wafer thickness of 635 μm (0.025 in) and a probe separation of 1587 μm (0.0625 in). This is the nominal separation of the probes being used for SRM certification, and the SRM wafers were, in fact, purchased with a target thickness of 625 μm. Some fraction of the wafers in a given SRM batch will exceed the ratio, 0.4, if only by a small amount, simply due to fabrication process tolerances. For the seven SRM levels, a total of 34 wafers (out of approximately 800) had thicknesses such that the t/S ratio exceeded 0.4; the worst-case value of the ratio was 0.4008.

Examination of the scaling factor shows that it actually has a value of 0.9995, not unity, for thickness-to-probe-spacing ratios that are infinitesimally above 0.4. When the procedure for

34

certification of these SRMs was devised, it was not known exactly how much variation in wafer-to-wafer thickness would be encountered. To avoid the inconsistency in scaling factor that would result from using a default value of unity for ratios up to 0.4, and then a calculated value of the scaling factor for all higher values of the ratio t/S, a decision was made to calculate and apply a correction term for all values of the thickness/probe separation ratio. The result is to improve the SRM wafer-to-wafer consistency for resistivity value as a function of thickness, but to introduce an offset for most SRM wafers that makes their stated resistivity 0.04 % to 0.05 % smaller than if the asymptotic value of unity had been used for this scaling factor. The exact amount of the offset for a given SRM wafer can be found, if needed, by comparing to unity the value of this scaling factor as printed on the certificate for that wafer. This offset is incorporated in both sheet resistance and resistivity values. There is no error, or uncertainty, term developed to relate to this change from the procedure of ASTM F84.

To calculate the variance in the scaling factor due to uncertainty in the measurements of thickness and probe separation, typical results for probe separation measurements and thickness data from one of the SRM levels are used. Following the procedures of ASTM F84, probe separations can be measured to a resolution of about 1 μm and with a typical precision for 10 readings of about 0.06 % (1 μm).

Wafer thickness and probe-spacing values for the 25 Ω·cm SRM level are used to calculate the variance of the wafer-thickness probe-spacing scaling factor. For this SRM level, the slightly larger upper end wafer thicknesses relative to the spacing of the probe used make the sensitivity of this term a little larger than for the other SRM levels. For this SRM, assuming no error in thickness or probe separation value, the ratio, t/S, ranges from 0.387 26 ($F(t/S) = 0.999$ 632), to 0.400 83 ($F(t/S) = 0.999$ 506). A worst-case combination of probe separation error (0.0002 cm assumed) and wafer thickness error (0.000 025 cm assumed) causes a change in the scaling factor value of about 0.000 03 (a relative change of 0.003 %). Using this value as a half-width (the error could also be the same amount in the opposite direction), and assuming a rectangular distribution, the variance of $F(t/s)$ is 5.07×10^{-10}. Thus, this contribution is negligible.

6. UNANTICIPATED EFFECTS

During the course of certification of the seven SRMs, two effects were encountered that had not been experienced previously and which were thus partially, or wholly, outside the design of the control experiments. The first of these was a shift, or drift, in measured resistivity during the first few rounds of probe measurements on the 200 Ω·cm SRMs. The second was a sensitivity of the measured resistivity to background illumination level for the 1 Ω·cm (SRM 2543) and the first batch of 10 Ω·cm (SRM 2544) wafers.

35

6.1 Resistivity Shift with Repeated Probing

The phenomenon of resistivity shift with repeated probing is documented in Sections 2.1 and 3.3 of the analysis of SRM 2547 which is given in Appendix 2. It shows up as a decrease of measured resistivity with successive sets of probe measurements made within a period of days or weeks. It was found to occur for some but not all wafers tested, and where it exists, it is stronger for some probes than for others. The shift is not totally cumulative, but appears to saturate.

Additional measurements of the original control wafers more than a year after the acquisition of the certification data showed nearly the same effect as shown in Appendix 2. The first of these additional measurements started at almost the same value as originally (i.e., an upward recovery of value had occurred in the interim), followed by a gradual decrease in resistivity by about the same amount as previously, then reached an asymptotic value. As previously noted, some of the control wafers suffered the effect; others did not. The observed shift did not accumulate beyond a few tenths of a percent.

The mechanism for this shift is unknown. It is not believed to be experienced with repeated eddy current measurements, but this hypothesis was not tested. It is expected that when wafers from SRM 2547 are first measured by the user, they will manifest the resistivity (sheet resistance) values listed on the certificate, and if measured by four-point probe, some of them will show small decreases of resistivity if replicate probe measurements are made within a period of days, or perhaps weeks. The additional term added to the estimated uncertainty interval due to analysis of this effect on the control wafers is believed to fully cover any manifestation of this effect to the user.

6.2 Photosensitivity of Resistivity Value

Measurements being made separately from the certification of these SRMs, and after the time when most of the SRMs had been measured for certification, showed that certain types of silicon had a resistivity value that was dependent on the level of background illumination. Extensive previous experience with four-probe measurements of many silicon specimens, particularly the types used for previous SRMs, had shown that normal laboratory-level fluorescent illumination had no observable effect on the measurement value. It had been seen that high resistivity silicon (perhaps 1000 $\Omega \cdot$cm, and higher) must be measured in the dark. It was also seen that bright incandescent illumination, with a significant component of penetrating infrared radiation, would inject hole-electron pairs that would decrease the measured resistivity with a very rapid recovery (because of short minority-carrier lifetimes) to higher values when that illumination was turned off.

Previous resistivity SRMs up to 200 $\Omega \cdot$cm, fabricated from float-zone or neutron-transmutation-doped silicon, showed no sensitivity of resistivity to normal laboratory levels of fluorescent lighting, and certification measurements were taken on them without a dark-box enclosure. The current 100 mm diameter SRM wafers were fabricated from boron-doped

Czochralski silicon from 0.01 $\Omega \cdot$cm to 10 $\Omega \cdot$cm and from float-zone grown, NTD-doped silicon for the highest three resistivity levels. These choices of silicon types were made specifically to optimize within-wafer uniformity of resistivity for the various SRM levels.

The photosensitivity of resistivity that was detected subsequent to SRM certification occurred on boron-doped Cz silicon wafers that were not related to the SRM wafers. Subsequent testing showed that the effect was measurable from a few tenths of an ohm centimeter to the highest resistivity boron-doped Cz silicon obtainable, approximately 80 $\Omega \cdot$cm. The magnitude of the shift in resistivity was found: 1) to be as high as 2.5 %, 2) to depend roughly on resistivity level, and 3) to be present on all boron-doped Cz silicon wafers available, independent of supplier and wafer surface type. Auxiliary tests, on wafers from the 1 $\Omega \cdot$cm and 10 $\Omega \cdot$cm SRM crystals, also showed a correlation between the magnitude of the effect and the interstitial oxygen level. The effect could not be detected at all on boron-doped float-zone silicon or on any phosphorus-doped silicon. Tests were then made of the existence and magnitude of this effect on wafers from the four boron-doped Cz silicon crystals that had already been certified for SRMs. No effect could be detected for the 0.01 $\Omega \cdot$cm or 0.1 $\Omega \cdot$cm resistivity levels. A photoeffect as large as 0.4 % and decreasing to about 0.15 %, as a function of wafer position in the starting crystal, was detected for wafers from SRM 2543, at 1 $\Omega \cdot$cm. The effect ranged from 0.6 % to 1.2 % for wafers from the crystal initially used for SRM 2544, at 10 $\Omega \cdot$cm.

The photosensitivity is unusual in its very long decay time from lower resistivity in normal room illumination to higher resistivity in the dark. Typical times for decay to the asymptotic value typical of the new illumination state ranged from about 2 min to more than 20 min. Wafers used for SRMs 2543 and 2544 were at the lower end of this time scale.

Because of the significantly large value of the photoeffect for wafers from the original 10 $\Omega \cdot$cm boron-doped Cz crystal, these wafers were invalidated for use as SRMs. It was possible to purchase a sufficient quantity of 10 $\Omega \cdot$cm wafers grown by the float-zone process and phosphorus-doped by the NTD technique to be able to retain the 10 $\Omega \cdot$cm SRM level using these replacement wafers. The NTD wafers are nearly as uniform as the boron-doped Cz silicon wafers they replaced and are suitable for use as SRMs since they show no evidence of a photosensitivity. The complete set of certification and control measurements have been completed on the NTD wafers. At the time of publication, analysis of those data is not complete.

The case for the 1 $\Omega \cdot$cm SRM level was not so straightforward. It was not possible to get float-zone grown, NTD-doped wafers that are irradiated heavily enough to produce 1 $\Omega \cdot$cm silicon. Possible replacement Cz silicon wafers doped with phosphorus were expected to be free of photosensitivity, but to have sufficiently large nonuniformity of resistivity as to be unacceptable for use as standards. No other alternative could be identified, and a choice had to be made between voiding the 1 $\Omega \cdot$cm SRM level altogether and a judicious use of the 1 $\Omega \cdot$cm wafers already measured. The decision was made to retain only the best of the original 1 $\Omega \cdot$cm SRM wafers, i.e., those wafers having the lowest amount of photosensitivity, about 0.25% and below. This will allow the retention of just over half of the originally measured batch of 125 wafers. The task of selection was made easy because the supplier for those wafers laser-engraved a unique serial number on each wafer in the sequence the wafers were taken from the saw. The magnitude of the photoeffect had been found to decrease monotonically from the low numbered toward the high numbered wafers.

During the analysis of the certification data for the 1 Ω·cm SRM, an estimate was made of a new component of uncertainty, due to the level of illumination. This estimate was based on measurements at normal operating illumination levels in the laboratory (ceiling fluorescent lights), measurements in the dark, and measurements at noticeably higher-than-normal levels of illumination. This latter condition served to evaluate shifts to lower values of resistivity that might occur in a user facility having a higher illumination level than was present in the NIST laboratory module during certification. A variety of sources of additional illumination were evaluated, and a two-cell flashlight with a krypton bulb flooding about a 5 cm. diameter an area, where the probe contacted the wafer, was chosen for the tests. This additional illumination caused saturation in the reduction of resistivity, but did not cause wafer heating. The results of the analysis of the photosensitivity effect, which were not available for the original issue of this report, are contained in Appendix 7 of this revision of the report.

Two notes of caution are in order regarding the use of moderate to lightly boron-doped Cz silicon wafers, regardless of source, for resistivity standards. Both are based on the assumption that photosensitivity, of the type described here, is a universal characteristic of boron-doped Cz silicon. First, it is not sufficient, in general, simply to take the certifying data in darkened surroundings. Any user of such a standard who is not able to take measurements in similarly darkened surroundings will experience a different resistivity value, and the difference between the dark-level and illuminated-level values may not be characterized adequately. Second, because the decay time for the photosensitivity is so long, it is relatively easy, using most commercial, automated instrumentation, to be fooled about whether a photosensitivity exists for a given wafer. Only a series of measurements over a period of minutes is likely to reveal the drift that is caused by this photosensitivity. There is a related consideration, for a wafer certified in the dark, that will be measured in a darkened, or shrouded, user-instrument, but which has been stored in illuminated surroundings. Such a wafer will have to be allowed to equilibrate with the darkened interior of the instrument for a number of minutes before valid readings can be taken.

7. COMPILATION OF UNCERTAINTY COMPONENTS

This section summarizes the Type A standard uncertainty terms for resistivity from Appendices 2 through 8 and the Type B variance terms from Section 5. It uses these inputs to obtain the combined variance, u_c^2, the combined standard uncertainty u_c, and the expanded uncertainty, U, for several parameters. The expanded uncertainty is stated on the SRM certificates for: 1) average resistivity at the wafer center; 2) average sheet resistance at the wafer center; and 3) individual sheet resistance measurements at locations on the 5 mm and 10 mm circles.

The values of Type A standard uncertainty in the appendices are given only for resistivity values. To convert these to values appropriate to sheet resistance, it is necessary only to divide them by the average SRM wafer thickness, 0.0628 cm. Separate values are needed for average sheet resistance at the wafer center and for individual measurements on the 5 mm and 10 mm radius circles. There are three considerations for converting the values of Type B variance of resistivity, given in Section 5, to values of variance of sheet resistance. First, since sheet resistance values do not depend on wafer thickness, only the terms in Section 5 from the variance of the electrical and temperature measurements contribute to Type B variance of sheet resistance. Second, Sections 5.2.2 and 5.2.3 give the contributions of electrical and temperature measurement variations to the variance of resistivity; it is necessary to divide those variance-of-resistivity terms by the square of the average SRM wafer thickness, ie. by $(0.0628 \text{ cm})^2$, to scale to the variance of sheet resistance. Third, the Type B variance terms are estimates of measurement scale error, and are the same for average measurements at the wafer-centers and for individual measurements on the two small circles.

7.1 Summary of Statistical Analysis Parameters from the Appendices

This section summarizes the information given in Appendices 2 through 8. It gives the symbols used in the statistical analyses, the components of Type A standard uncertainty that they represent, and a table of values obtained for these components for five of the SRM levels. It also gives a summary of the Type A standard uncertainty values for wafer-center averages and for individual values on the 5 mm and 10 mm radius circles for both resistivity and sheet resistance. The nominal resistivity for each of the SRMs is given in Table 1 of Appendix 1.

Table 6. Components Identified in Statistical Analyses of Certification
and Control Experiment Data

The general form for the Type A standard uncertainty for the certification of these resistivity SRMs is:

$$u_i = \left(s_\varepsilon^2 / n + s_\delta^2 + s_\gamma^2 + s_c^2 + s_\Delta^2 + s_{cfig}^2 + a^2/3 + b^2/3 + c^2/3 \right)^{1/2}$$

where n = 1 for individual measurements on the circles and n = 6 for the average value at the center, and

s_ε Short-term imprecision of certification probe

s_δ Run-to-run measurement variability

s_γ Longer-term measurement variability

s_c Uncertainty of non-zero correction for bias of certification probe

s_Δ Uncertainty of non-zero correction for probing induced drift (wafer-probe interaction)

s_{cfig} Uncertainty of non-zero correction for probe-wiring configuration difference

$a/\sqrt{3}$ Uncertainty of correction for probe wiring configuration (where the best correction = 0)
          [Type A estimate, but based on limit of error]

$b/\sqrt{3}$ Uncertainty of correction for bias of certification probe (where the best correction = 0)
          [Type A estimate, but based on limit of error]

$c/\sqrt{3}$ Uncertainty of correction for effect of illumination level (where the best correction = 0)
          [Type A estimate, but based on limit of error].

Table 7. Values of the Components Identified in Statistical Analyses for the various SRMs
in Appendices 2 through 8 and 10 through 12, $m\Omega \cdot cm$* #

SRM	S_ε	S_δ	S_γ	S_ζ	S_Δ	S_{cfig}	$a/\sqrt{3}$	$b/\sqrt{3}$	$c/\sqrt{3}$
2541	0.001 83	0.001 04	0.004 00	0.	0.	0.000 01	0.	0.000 47	0
2541b2	0.002 32	0.001 04	0.001 17	0.	0.	0.000 19	0.	0.000 64	0
2542	0.062	0.032	0.004	0.	0.011	0.	0.	0.016	0
2543	0.714	0.192	0.154	0.	0.	0.058	0.	0.038	1.682
2543b2	0.552	0.206	0.	0	0.	0.024	0	0.009	1.262
2544	4.662	1.198	5.646	0.	0.	0.287	0.	0.204	0
2544b2	4.666	1.095	0.0	0.26	0.	0.	0.	0.	0
2545	14.14	3.31	3.01	0.	0.	0.	2.89	0.	0
2546	72.0	13.4	14.6	5.1	0.	0.	0.	0.	0
2547	138.	64.	129.	5.	10.	0.	0.	0.	0

*For ease of reading, this table is expressed in terms of milliohm centimeters whereas in the individual appendices the uncertainty components are expressed in ohm centimeters.

 # Appendices 2-8 are in the sequence in which the SRMs were completed, not in the order of resistivity level

Entries for 2541b2, 2543b2 and 2544b2, in this table and those following indicate " second batch" certifications for these SRMs, with new control measurements and Type A uncertainty analyses for each of them (Type B uncertainty components remain unchanged from the first batch, "batch 1" of these SRMs). The revised certificates for the second batches are dated as follows:

   2544b2: Sept 6, 2002; 2541b2: Jan 6, 2003; 2543b2: June 15, 2004.

For the serial numbers to which these revised, batch 2, analyses and certificates apply, see Appendix 13.

Table 8. Type A Standard Uncertainty Values, u_i, Taken from Reports in Appendices 2 to 8 and 10 to 12

SRM	RESISTIVITY at center ($m\Omega \cdot em$)	RESISTIVITY on circles ($m\Omega \cdot em$)	SHEET RESISTANCE at center ($m\Omega$)	SHEET RESISTANCE on circles ($m\Omega$)
2541	$\pm 0.004\ 23$	± 0.0045	$\pm 0.067\ 3$	± 0.0716
2541b2	$\pm 0.001\ 95$	± 0.0029	± 0.0310	± 0.0460
2542	± 0.045	± 0.072	± 0.725	± 1.16
2543	± 1.72	± 1.85	± 27.5	± 29.6
2543b2	± 1.30	± 1.39	± 20.77	± 22.29
2544	± 6.09	± 7.43	± 96.9	± 118.3
2544b2	± 2.03	± 4.72	± 32.3	± 75.2
2545	± 7.8	± 15.1	$\pm 125.$	$\pm 241.$
2546	± 35.8	± 74.8	$\pm 570.$	$\pm 1190.$
2547	$\pm 155.$	$\pm 199.$	$\pm 2470.$	$\pm 3180.$

Type A and Type B Variance Terms

In this section, Table 9 gives the variance terms constructed from the squares of the Type A standard uncertainty values listed in Table 8. Table 10 gives Type B variance values, obtained from the analyses in Section 5. Finally, Table 11 gives the combined variance, u^2_c, obtained by adding the Type A and Type B variances.

Table 9. Type A Variance Values, u^2_i, Obtained by Squaring the Entries in Table 8

SRM	RESISTIVITY at center $(\Omega \cdot cm)^2$	RESISTIVITY on circles $(\Omega \cdot cm)^2$	SHEET RESISTANCE at center (Ω^2)	SHEET RESISTANCE on circles (Ω^2)
2541	1.79×10^{-11}	2.02×10^{-11}	4.53×10^{-9}	5.13×10^{-9}
2541b2	3.80×10^{-12}	8.41×10^{-12}	9.61×10^{-10}	2.12×10^{-9}
2542	2.02×10^{-9}	5.18×10^{-9}	5.26×10^{-7}	1.35×10^{-6}
2543	2.96×10^{-6}	3.42×10^{-6}	7.57×10^{-4}	8.76×10^{-4}
2543b2	1.68×10^{-6}	1.93×10^{-6}	4.31×10^{-4}	4.97×10^{-4}
2544	3.71×10^{-5}	5.52×10^{-5}	9.40×10^{-3}	1.40×10^{-2}
2544b2	4.12×10^{-6}	2.23×10^{-5}	1.04×10^{-3}	5.66×10^{-3}
2545	6.08×10^{-5}	2.28×10^{-4}	1.56×10^{-2}	5.81×10^{-2}
2546	1.28×10^{-3}	5.59×10^{-3}	3.25×10^{-1}	1.42
2547	2.40×10^{-2}	3.96×10^{-2}	6.10	10.1

Table 10. Type B Variance Values, u^2_j, Calculated from Summation of Terms in Section 5.2 *

SRM	RESISTIVITY at center & on circles $(\Omega \cdot cm)^2$	SHEET RESISTANCE at center & on circles (Ω^2)
2541	2.51×10^{-11}	5.68×10^{-9}
2541b2	2.51×10^{-11}	5.68×10^{-9}
2542	8.68×10^{-10}	1.51×10^{-7}
2543	1.84×10^{-7}	3.96×10^{-5}
2543b2	1.84×10^{-7}	3.96×10^{-5}
2544	2.32×10^{-5}	5.18×10^{-3}
2544b2	2.32×10^{-5}	5.18×10^{-3}
2545	1.47×10^{-4}	3.30×10^{-2}
2546	2.36×10^{-3}	5.28×10^{-1}
2547	9.43×10^{-3}	2.11

* Type B variance components are the same for batches 1 and 2 of SRMs 2541, 2543 and 2544

Table 11. Combined Variance Values, u^2_c, from Addition of Terms in Tables 9 and 10

SRM	RESISTIVITY at center $(\Omega \cdot cm)^2$	RESISTIVITY on circles $(\Omega \cdot cm)^2$	SHEET RESISTANCE at center (Ω^2)	SHEET RESISTANCE on circles (Ω^2)
2541	4.30×10^{-11}	4.53×10^{-11}	1.02×10^{-8}	1.08×10^{-8}
2541b2	2.89×10^{-11}	3.35×10^{-11}	6.64×10^{-9}	7.80×10^{-9}
2542	2.89×10^{-9}	6.05×10^{-9}	6.77×10^{-7}	1.50×10^{-6}
2543	3.14×10^{-6}	3.61×10^{-6}	7.97×10^{-4}	9.16×10^{-4}

2543b2	1.86×10^{-6}	2.11×10^{-6}	4.71×10^{-4}	5.37×10^{-4}
2544	6.03×10^{-5}	7.84×10^{-5}	1.46×10^{-2}	1.92×10^{-2}
2544b2	2.73×10^{-5}	4.55×10^{-5}	6.23×10^{-3}	1.08×10^{-2}
2545	2.08×10^{-4}	3.75×10^{-4}	4.86×10^{-2}	9.11×10^{-2}
2546	3.64×10^{-3}	7.95×10^{-3}	8.53×10^{-1}	1.95
2547	3.35×10^{-2}	4.90×10^{-2}	8.21	12.2

Standard Uncertainty and Expanded Uncertainty

Table 12 gives values of the combined standard uncertainty, u_c, and Table 13 gives the expanded uncertainty, U, based on a coverage factor $k = 2$ where $U = k\,u_c$. The combined standard uncertainty values are the square roots of the combined variance entries in Table 11.

Table 12. Combined Standard Uncertainty Values, u_c

SRM	RESISTIVITY at center (Ω·cm)	RESISTIVITY on circles (Ω·cm)	SHEET RESISTANCE at center (Ω)	SHEET RESISTANCE on circles (Ω)
2541	±0.000 006 56	±0.000 006 73	±0.000 101	±0.000 104
2541b2	±0.000 005 38	±0.000 005 79	±0.000 081	±0.000 088
2542	±0.000 0538	±0.000 077 8	±0.000 823	±0.001 22
2543	±0.001 77	±0.001 90	±0.0282	±0.0303
2543b2	±0.001 36	±0.001 45	±0.0217	±0.0232
2544	±0.007 76	±0.008 85	±0.1208	±0.1385
2544b2	±0.005 22	±0.006 74	±0.0789	±0.1039
2545	±0.0144	±0.0194	±0.220	±0.302
2546	±0.0603	±0.0892	±0.924	±1.39
2547	±0.183	±0.221	±2.86	±3.49

Table 13. Expanded Uncertainty Values, U (Coverage Factor $k = 2$)

SRM	RESISTIVITY at center (Ω·cm)	RESISTIVITY on circles (Ω·cm)	SHEET RESISTANCE at center (Ω)	SHEET RESISTANCE on circles (Ω)
2541	0.000 013 1	0.000 013 5	0.000 202	0.000 208
2541b2	0.000 010 8	0.000 011 6	0.000 163	0.000 177
2542	0.000 108	0.000 156	0.001 65	0.002 45
2543	0.003 54	0.003 80	0.0564	0.0605
2543b2	0.002 73	0.002 90	0.0434	0.0464
2544	0.015 53	0.017 70	0.241	0.277
2544b2	0.0104	0.0135	0.1578	0.2078
2545	0.0288	0.0387	0.441	0.604
2546	0.121	0.178	1.85	2.78
2547*	-0.498, +0.366	-0.575, +0.443	-7.83, +5.73	-9.08, +6.98

* Asymmetry is due to a contribution of 0.132 Ω·cm, 2.10 Ω, from a wafer-probe interaction, i.e., a drift in value with repeated probing.

42

7.2 Corrections Applied to Measured Values

This section summarizes bias corrections that must be made to measurement results, as acquired, because of effects that were identified during statistical analyses of the SRM certification experiment data. These corrections are explained in the appropriate appendices. They are given for resistivity and sheet resistance values. **All resistivity and sheet resistance values shown on the SRM certificates have already been corrected for these bias terms.**

Table 14. Probe Bias Corrections Applied to Measured Values

SRM	BIAS CORRECTION to Resistivity (Sheet resistance)		SOURCE
2541	Subtract 0.000 000 472 Ω·cm	(0.000 007 52 Ω)	Wiring Configuration Bias
	[This is a Negligible Amount]		
2541b2	Subtract 0.000 002 14 Ω·cm	(0.000 034 08 Ω)	Wiring Configuration Bias
2542	Subtract 0.000 037 5 Ω·cm	(0.000 597 Ω)	Wiring Configuration Bias
2543	Subtract 0.000 131 Ω·cm	(0.002 10 Ω)	Wiring Configuration Bias
2543b2	Subtract 0.000 25 Ω·cm	(0.004 00 Ω)	Wiring Configuration Bias
2544	Subtract 0.0011 Ω·cm	(0.017 Ω)	Wiring Configuration Bias
2544b2	Subtract 0.000 816 Ω·cm	(0.0130 Ω)	Probe Bias
2545	None		----------------------------
2546	Add 0.0393 Ω·cm	(0.626 Ω)	Probe Bias
2547	Subtract 0.0490 Ω·cm	(0.78 Ω)	Probe Bias
	[a wafer drift term of 0.132 Ω·cm, (2.10 Ω), is built into expanded uncertainty for SRM 2547]		

7.5 Estimated Degrees of Freedom for Uncertainty Values of the SRMs

Table 15 summarizes the estimated degrees of freedom for the stated uncertainty values of each of the SRMs. These estimates are made using the Welch-Satterthwaite formula [5]. They can be used to estimate the confidence interval covered by the expanded uncertainties with coverage factor $k = 2$. The wide variation in the degrees of freedom listed arises from the difference in the number of degrees of freedom for the dominant effect contributing to the uncertainty of each of the SRMs.

Table 15. Estimate of Degrees of Freedom from the Welch-Satterthwaite Formula

SRM	Center Average Degrees of Freedom	Individual Measurement Degrees of Freedom
2541	6	8
2541b2	24	109
2542	88	486
2543	16800	15415
2543b2	25820	21512
2544	6	14
2544b2	68	607
2545	52	528
2546	41	543
2547	26	66

43

8. CONCLUSION

When the certification procedure for the SRMs was being developed, the quantitative design objective was to support the goal for layer resistivity stated in the SEMATECH Mega-IC Workshop, i.e., measurements with a 1% accuracy and a 0.5% repeatability. NIST and ISO practice is to state the total uncertainty of measurement values, rather than to state accuracy and precision values separately. However, values of expanded uncertainty, listed in Table 13, can be used to give a reasonable assessment of how well the design objectives for this SRM series were met. Values of expanded uncertainty for resistivity averages at the center of an SRM wafer range from 0.11% to 0.25%, of the nominal resistivity for all SRMs except 2543 at 1 $\Omega\cdot$cm; for this SRM the expanded uncertainty is 0.35%. The relative uncertainty of individual resistivity values on the two circles increases slightly for several resistivity levels where probe imprecision was one of the larger contributors to uncertainty, but it is still less than 0.2% for five of the SRM levels and is 0.38% at 1 $\Omega\cdot$cm and 0.28% at 200 $\Omega\cdot$cm. Expanded uncertainties for sheet resistance values are slightly smaller since there is no uncertainty due to thickness scale in the sheet resistance values. Thus, these SRMs should serve quite well to support the original design goals.

9. ACKNOWLEDGMENTS

It is a happy privilege to acknowledge the dedication and persistence of Donnie Ricks throughout all the preliminary testing, the certification, and follow-up testing that was necessary for the certification of these SRMs. Without her conscientious attention to detail, the uncertainty levels noted in the report could not have been achieved. Thanks also to Mike Thomas for his able assistance throughout the certification. A special thank you goes to Jane Walters for her diligent and meticulous work in preparing this report from a number of disparate-format pieces of source material.

REFERENCES

[1]   ASTM Method F84-93, "Standard Method for Measuring Resistivity of Silicon Wafers with an In-Line Four-Point Probe, " Annual Book of ASTM Standards Vol. 10.05, West Conshohocken, PA 19428.

[2]   Recommendations for Specific Standards Actions, Proceedings of the SEMATECH Workshop on Silicon Materials for Mega-IC Applications, New Orleans, Louisiana, January 30-31, 1991, p.9.

[3]   van der Pauw, L.J., A Method of Measuring Specific Resistivity and Hall Effect of Discs of Arbitrary Shape, Phil. Res. Rep. 13, 1-9 (1958).

[4]   Guide to the Expression of Uncertainty in Measurement, ISBN 92-67-10188-9, 1st Ed. ISO, Geneva, Switzerland, (1993).

[5]   Taylor, B.N. and Kuyatt, C. E., Guidelines for Evaluating and Expressing the Uncertainty of NIST Measurement Results, NIST Technical Note 1297, U.S. Government Printing Office, Washington DC (1994).

[6]   ASTM Method F1529-96, "Standard Method for Sheet Resistance Uniformity Evaluation by In-Line Four-Point Probe with the Dual-Configuration Procedure," Annual Book of ASTM Standards Vol. 10.05, West Conshohocken, PA 19428.

[7]   Harris, F. K., Electrical Measurements (John Wiley & Sons, New York, 1952), p. 431.

[8]   Perloff, D. S., Gan, J. N. and Wahl, F. E., Dose Accuracy and Doping Uniformity of Ion Implant Equipment, Solid State Technol. 24 (2), 112-120 (1981).

[9]   Perloff, D. S., Four-Point Probe Correction Factors for Use in Measuring Large Diameter Doped Semiconductor Wafers, J. Electrochem Soc. 123 (11), 1745-1750 (1977).

Appendix 1. Summary of Important SRM Wafer Material
and Measurement Condition Parameters

This appendix consists of two tables that summarize important useful silicon wafer characteristics and electrical measurement conditions that apply to the various resistivity levels of SRMs 2541 to 2547. Table 1 lists the nominal resistivity, crystallographic orientation of the SRM wafer surfaces, crystal growth type, dopant species, and the commercial supplier for the wafers for each of the SRMs. Table 2 lists the four-point probe identification, the serial number and nominal resistance of the standard resistor used, as well as the nominal value of the measurement current used for certification of these same SRMs.

Table 1. Silicon Wafer Characteristics That Apply to Various Resistivity Levels of the SRMs 2541 to 2547

SRM	SRM level (in $\Omega \cdot cm$)	Crystal	Orient/Growth/Dopant	Supplier
2541	0.01	91905	(100) Cz Boron	Recticon Corp.
2542	0.1	91904	(100) Cz Boron	Recticon Corp.
2543	1	91907	(100) Cz Boron	Recticon Corp.
2544	10	29473	(111) FZ-NTD Phos.	Wacker Siltronic
2545	25	21565	(111) FZ-NTD Phos.	Topsil Semi. A/S
2546	100	51939	(111) FZ-NTD Phos.	Topsil Semi. A/S
2547	200	21566	(111) FZ-NTD Phos.	Topsil Semi. A/S

Table 2. Electrical Measurement Conditions That Apply to Various Resistivity Levels of the SRMs 2541 to 2547

SRM	Probe	Standard Resistor Nominal Value/ Serial Number	Nominal Measurement Current	
2541	283	0.1 Ω / 1771494	100	mA
2542	281	1 Ω / 1594503	28	mA
2543	283	10 Ω / 1593079	2.8	mA
2544	283	100 Ω / 1598893	260	μA
2545	2062	100 Ω / 1598893	110	μA
2546	2362	1000 Ω / 1592167	29	μA
2547	SRM1	1000 Ω / 1592167	14	μA

Appendix 2. Analysis of Certification Data
and Control Experiments for SRM 2547

1. GENERAL COMMENTS AND SUMMARY OF TYPE A STANDARD UNCERTAINTY COMPONENTS

1.1 Introduction

This appendix documents the statistical analysis leading to the certification of wafers from crystal 21566 for SRM 2547 and outlines a general procedure for analysis of other SRMs in the series 2541 through 2547. The results of the analyses of the remaining SRMs are briefly summarized in the following appendices. In addition to the three random components and the first three systematic components listed below which are common to all SRMs, this report also treats a small drift effect that was not found with any of the other SRMs.

The 137 wafers in this issue have nominal resistivities of 200 $\Omega\cdot$cm, and the wafers are assumed to be identical with regard to wafer face. Certification measurements are made with a single probe, identified as SRM1. Data consist of measurements at six locations on each of three circles located at 0 mm, 5 mm, and 10 mm from the center of each wafer, with the wafer face chosen at random with respect to the crystal growth direction. Sources of error which could contribute to the uncertainties of the certified values and which are examined in this appendix are: probe imprecision, run-to-run variability, long-term variability, differences between wiring configurations, differences between wafer faces, differences among probes (probe SRM1 bias), and wafer drift with probing, which was an unanticipated effect.

Only the standard deviation associated with probe spacing and electronic imprecision can be estimated from the certification data for the SRM wafers. A series of control experiments was carried out to identify and estimate error components which cannot be addressed by the certification measurements.

Measurements on a check-standard, chosen at random from the wafers in the issue, were made routinely during the certification procedure to: identify any anomalous behavior, document the stability of the process, and estimate a day-to-day component of measurement error. For this issue, the check standard is wafer #150; it was measured only with the certification probe SRM1.

Pre- and post-certification control experiments with five probes on five wafers with both second-configurations, b1 and b2, were repeated on 6 days. These measurements are intended to estimate both the random and systematic components of the measurement process. The next section summarizes the Type A standard uncertainty for SRM 2547. It also gives a statement of how the uncorrected term due to wafer drift contributes to the expanded uncertainty. Tables 1 and 2 in Section 1.2 give an executive summary of the terms that contribute to the Type A standard uncertainty. The details of the calculation of the component terms are given in subsequent sections.

1.2 Certified Resistivities and Uncertainties

The average of six measurements on the 0 mm circle of each wafer, corrected for the effect of probe SRM1, is reported as the certified resistivity value. The Type A standard uncertainty associated with the certified value for the wafer center is

$$u_i = \left(s_c^2 + s_\gamma^2 + s_\delta^2 + \frac{1}{6} s_\epsilon^2 + s_\Delta^2\right)^{1/2} = 0.155 \ \Omega \cdot cm .$$

The expanded uncertainty (coverage factor k = 2) allows for an uncorrected systematic error of -Δ. See Section 3.3 for details. Because the uncorrected systematic error is always in one direction, the expanded uncertainty interval is nonsymmetric and is expressed as

$$Certified \ value - (2 \ u_i + \Delta), \ Certified \ value + 2 \ u_i ,$$

where $2 \ u_i = 0.310 \ \Omega \cdot cm$, and $\Delta = 0.132 \ \Omega \cdot cm$.

Individual measurements on the 5 mm and 10 mm circles for each wafer, corrected for the effect of probe SRM1, are reported as certified values on the certificates. The Type A standard uncertainty associated with each of these individual certified values is

$$u_i = \left(s_c^2 + s_\gamma^2 + s_\delta^2 + s_\epsilon^2 + s_\Delta^2\right)^{1/2} = 0.20 \ \Omega \cdot cm .$$

The expanded uncertainty interval for individual measurements is then expressed by

$$Certified \ value - (2 \ u_i + \Delta), \ Certified \ value + 2 \ u_i ,$$

where $2 \ u_i$ for individual measurements $= 0.40 \ \Omega \cdot cm.$

Table 1. Components of Type A Standard Uncertainty for Crystal 21566, SRM 2547 with Probe SRM1, $\Omega\cdot$cm

Type	Source	Std dev	Estimate
Random	Imprecision of probe SRM1	s_ε	0.138
Random	Run-to-run measurement variability	s_δ	0.064
Random	Long-term measurement variability	s_γ	0.129
Random	Standard deviation of correction for probe SRM1 bias*	s_c	0.005
Random	Standard deviation of wafer drift with probing	s_Δ	0.010
Systematic	Difference between configurations b1 and b2		Negligible
Systematic	Difference between front and back faces of wafer		Negligible
Systematic	Neglected correction for wafer drift with probing	Δ	0.132

* A correction of -0.049 $\Omega\cdot$cm due to probe SRM1 bias is applied to wafer center resistivity data for all wafers.

Table 2. Sources of Variation for Crystal 21566, SRM 2547 with Probe SRM1, Ω·cm

Source of error	Experiment	RMSE[a]	DF[b]	Relationship[c]
Probe imprecision	SRM certifications	0.1374	685	s_ε
	Pre-certification	0.1586	150	
	Post-certification	0.1134	150	
	Check standard	0.1367	105	
	Pooled	0.138	1090	
Run-to-run	Pre-certification	0.0857	20	$(s_\delta^2 + \frac{1}{6}s_\varepsilon^2)^{1/2}$
	Post-certification	0.0926	20	
	Check standard	0.0772	20	
	Pooled	0.0854	60	
Long-term	Pre- and post-certification	0.1116	5	$(s_\gamma^2 + \frac{1}{5}s_\delta^2 + \frac{1}{30}s_\varepsilon^2)^{1/2}$
	#900 wafers	0.1477	8	
	Pooled	0.1350	13	

[a]The root-mean-square error, RMSE, estimates within each source-of-error category are pooled in the table above. Standard deviations associated with the individual effects, namely, imprecision, run-to-run variability, probe variability, and long-term variability, are computed using the relationship shown in the last column, with the results summarized in Table 1 of this Appendix.
[b]Degree of Freedom.
[c]This column expresses the error components that comprise the pooled value in each "source of error" series of experiments; see reference at end of this Appendix.

2. RANDOM COMPONENTS

2.1 Pre- and Post-Certification Control Experiments

A nested experiment was performed with five probes on five wafers. Six measurements were made at the center position of each wafer with each probe; this sequence was repeated on 6 days; and the entire experiment was conducted twice, i.e., prior to and at the conclusion of the certification experiment. The temporal error model for one probe and one wafer is

$$y_{ijk} = \mu + \gamma_i + \delta_{ij} + \varepsilon_{ijk} \qquad i = 1,2; \; j = 1, ..., 6; \; k = 1, ... ,6 \qquad (1)$$

where μ is the average value, γ_i is a component for long-term error; δ_{ij} is a component of run-to-run measurement error; and ε_{ijk} represents short-term measurement imprecision error associated with the probe and electronics.

For this SRM, the pre- and post-certification measurements were made on opposite faces of the same wafers. Thus, there is a question as to whether the differences (see Fig. 1) between the pre- and post-certification measurements are caused by: (1) biases between faces; (2) drift on the wafer surfaces; or (3) long-term error in the measurement process.

1) Because the faces for the pre-certification experiment were chosen at random, it is unlikely that the differences, which are consistently in one direction, are caused by a front-to-back bias on the wafers. See Figure 1 where resistivity measurements on the five wafers are plotted versus the month/day of measurement. Also, measurements made 2 to 3 months after the conclusion of the certification process on additional wafers called #901, #902, #903, and #904 show differences which are consistently in the opposite direction.

2) There are not sufficient data from these experiments to judge inherent wafer drift.

3) The behavior of the pre- and post-certification data, which show strong correlations across wafers with time, is consistent with a components of variance model such as eq (1).

Sources of error and root-mean-square error terms (RMSE) for this model are in Table 2. For analysis of the initial and final control experiments, the first day's measurements were omitted. Estimates are made for each wafer individually and then pooled over wafers. The last column of the table shows the relationships between the results of the various experiments and the terms in the temporal error model above.

51

Crystal 21566

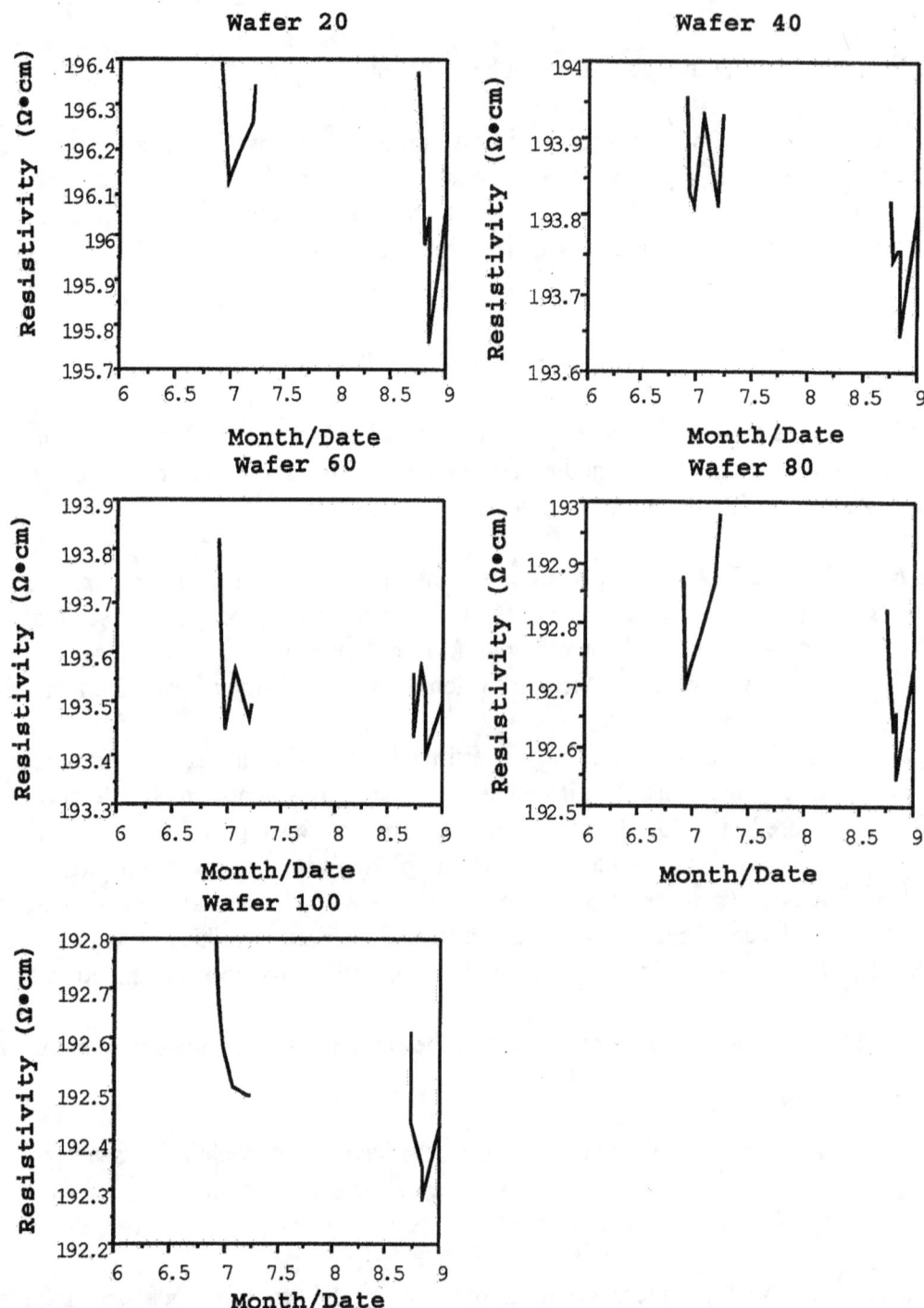

Figure 1. Resistivity (Ω·cm) on five control-wafers from crystal 21566 with probe SRM1 plotted versus the month/day of measurement, showing change between and within pre- and post-certification experiments.

2.1.1 Precision of probes

The standard deviation, s_ε, is directly computed from six measurements at the center and estimates the precision for each probe. These standard deviations are shown in Table 3; the pooled values are also shown in Table 2.

Table 3. Within-Run Standard Deviations, s_ε, Pooled over Five Wafers
and Six Runs, Ω·cm

	Probe	Std. dev, s_ε Config b1	DF	Std. dev, s_ε Config b2	DF
	SRM1	**0.1586**	**150**	**0.1907**	**150**
	281	0.2235	150	0.2468	150
Pre	283	0.2139	150	0.2389	150
	2062	0.1645	150	0.2043	150
	2362	0.1520	150	0.1635	150
	SRM1	**0.1134**	**150**	**0.1280**	**150**
	281	0.2102	150	0.2217	150
Post	283	0.1687	150	0.2115	150
	2062	0.1568	150	0.1770	150
	2362	0.1269	150	0.1374	150
Pooled Value:	SRM1	0.1379	300	0.1624	300

2.1.2 Run-to-run measurement variability from pre- and post-certification control experiments

Standard deviations and averages computed from the six repetitions with each probe on each wafer are shown in Table 4. For this purpose, the first run with each probe on each wafer has been discarded. Each standard deviation is then estimated with four degrees of freedom. The pooled standard deviation for SRM1 of 0.089 20 Ω·cm with 40 degrees of freedom incorporates both probe imprecision and day-to-day measurement error as shown in the relationship column of Table 2.

Table 4. Run-to-Run Component of Error, Crystal 21566
Averages and Standard Deviations for Last Five Runs
on Each Control-Wafer, $\Omega \cdot$cm

Wafer#	Probe	Pre-certification		Post-certification	
		Average	Std dev	Average	Std dev
20	SRM1	196.2431	0.0875	196.0078	0.1574
40	SRM1	193.8663	0.0615	193.7433	0.0605
60	SRM1	193.5259	0.0795	193.4869	0.0693
80	SRM1	192.8096	0.1127	192.6597	0.0777
100	SRM1	192.5503	0.0835	192.3768	0.0596
20	281	196.2443	0.1380	196.0423	0.2617
40	281	193.8445	0.1105	193.7325	0.0948
60	281	193.5903	0.0935	193.4285	0.1399
80	281	192.7595	0.0826	192.6768	0.1939
100	281	192.5428	0.1189	192.3991	0.0930
20	283	196.1670	0.0937	195.9598	0.1525
40	283	193.7223	0.0499	193.6426	0.0951
60	283	193.4253	0.0536	193.3253	0.0992
80	283	192.7630	0.0396	192.5120	0.0945
100	283	192.4705	0.0545	192.3259	0.0824
20	2062	196.1481	0.1042	195.9211	0.2248
40	2062	193.8217	0.0957	193.7494	0.0711
60	2062	193.4647	0.0723	193.4411	0.0355
80	2062	192.7436	0.0727	192.6205	0.1538
100	2062	192.4263	0.0412	192.3818	0.0644
20	2362	196.1432	0.0884	195.8630	0.2282
40	2362	193.7696	0.0681	193.7181	0.0667
60	2362	193.4426	0.0581	193.3722	0.0775
80	2362	192.7206	0.0920	192.5816	0.0810
100	2362	192.4557	0.1279	192.2694	0.1589
Pooled Value:	SRM1		0.085 73		0.092 55

2.1.3 Long-term measurement variability from the control-wafers

Averages for each wafer from the pre- and post-certification experiments are shown in Table 5. The differences are assumed to be the result of a long-term component of measurement error. The standard deviations as estimated from the pre- and post-certification averages represent probe imprecision, day-to-day error, and long-term measurement error as shown in the relationships column of Table 2.

Table 5. Pre- and Post-Certification Averages with Probe SRM1, Ω·cm

Wafer[#]	Pre-Certification	Post-Certification	Difference	Std dev	DF
20	196.2431	196.0078	-0.2353	0.1664	1
40	193.8663	193.7433	-0.1230	0.0870	1
60	193.5259	193.4869	-0.0390	0.0276	1
80	192.8096	192.6597	-0.1499	0.1060	1
100	192.5503	192.3768	-0.1735	0.1227	1
Pooled Value:				0.1116	5

2.1.4 Long-term measurement error from #900 series wafers

Averages of six center measurements made 2 to 3 months after the certification procedure are shown in Table 6. The measurements were made on a random selection of additional wafers numbered #901, #902, #903, and #904. The differences are assumed to be the result of a long-term component of measurement error. The standard deviations as estimated from the September and October averages represent probe imprecision, day-to-day error, and long-term measurement error as shown in the relationships column of Table 2. The fact that the differences shown in Table 5 for the control-wafers are always negative, whereas the differences observed for the #900 series of wafers are nearly always positive, is taken to indicate that this is not an inherent systematic effect. Therefore, no systematic correction term is applied.

Table 6. Long-Term Changes in Measurement Process with SRM1, Ω·cm

Wafer	Face	September	October	Difference	Std dev	DF
901	1	192.748	192.839	+0.091	0.0643	1
902	1	195.654	195.593	-0.061	0.0431	1
903	1	200.866	201.096	+0.230	0.1626	1
904	1	190.982	191.381	+0.399	0.2821	1
901	2	192.704	192.974	+0.270	0.1909	1
902	2	195.478	195.533	+0.055	0.0389	1
903	2	200.955	201.098	+0.143	0.1011	1
904	2	191.198	191.367	+0.169	0.1195	1
Pooled Value:					0.1477	8

2.2 Check-Standard Measurements

Twenty-three measurements (averages of six center measurements each) with probe SRM1 on wafer #150 were made over the course of the certification experiment. The initial drop in resistivity after the first day, which can be seen in Figure 2, is assumed to be the result of wafer-probing damage. The first day's measurements are omitted from the analysis. The slope of a straight line fit to the remaining 21 measurements as a function of time is not significant, indicating that the measurement process is not drifting. Therefore, only run-to-run variations in the measurement process and probe imprecision are reflected in the standard deviation which is shown in Table 2.

Crystal 21566

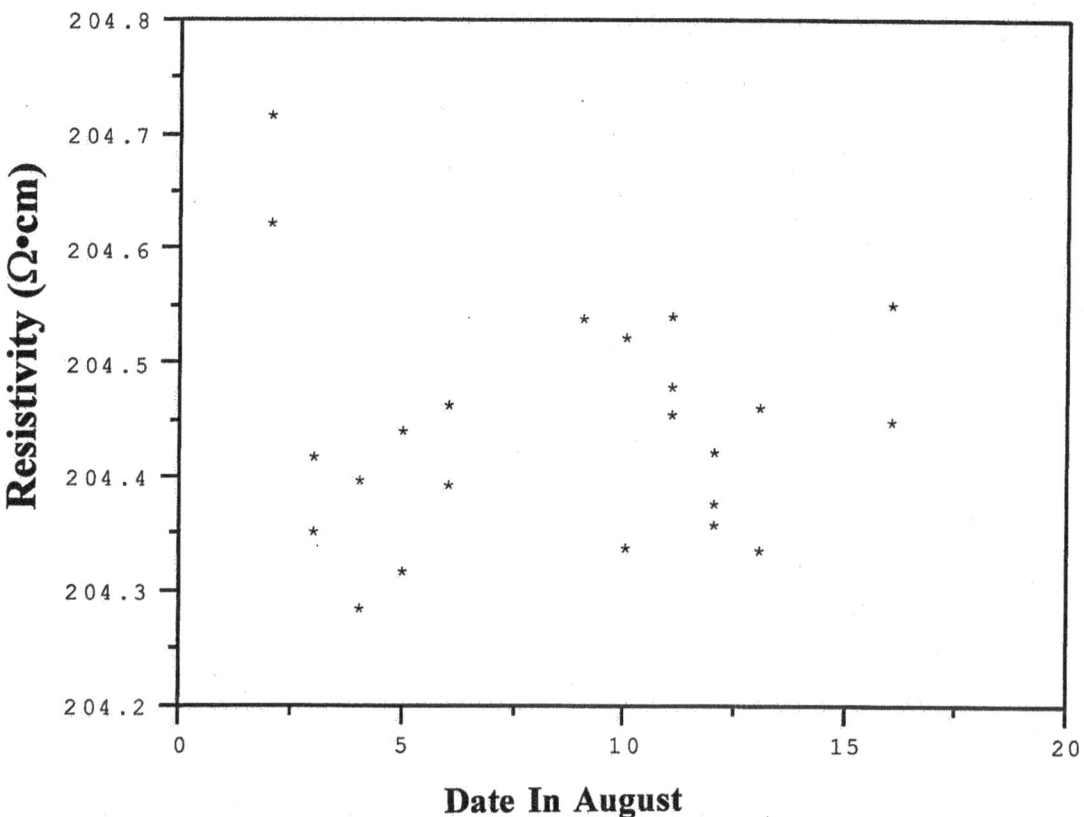

Figure 2. Resistivity measurements ($\Omega \cdot$cm) on check-wafer #150, with probe SRM1 as a function of time (date in August)

3. SYSTEMATIC COMPONENTS

3.1 Systematic Differences between Probe-Wiring Configurations b1 and b2

In the pre- and post-certification experiments, six measurements at the center with the probe in configuration b1 were immediately followed by six measurements with the probe in configuration b2. The differences between configurations b1 and b2 for the pre- and post-certification measurements are shown in Figure 3. Averages and standard deviations for each probe over 6 days and five wafers are shown in Table 7. The t-statistic,

$$t = \sqrt{30} \ \ \text{Average/Std dev} ,$$

shows no evidence of a significant difference between configurations b1 and b2 for the pre-certification measurements and some evidence of a difference for the post-certification measurements. These differences for the post-certification measurements appear to be caused by the measurements on the first two wafers. No uncertainty from this source is assigned.

Table 7. Average Differences over All Control-Wafers
between Configurations b1 and b2 for Probe SRM1, $\Omega \cdot$cm

Probe	Pre-certification			Post-certification		
	Average	Std dev	DF	Average	Std dev	DF
SRM1	-0.002 44	0.044 49	29	0.020 56	0.031 38	29

Crystal 21566

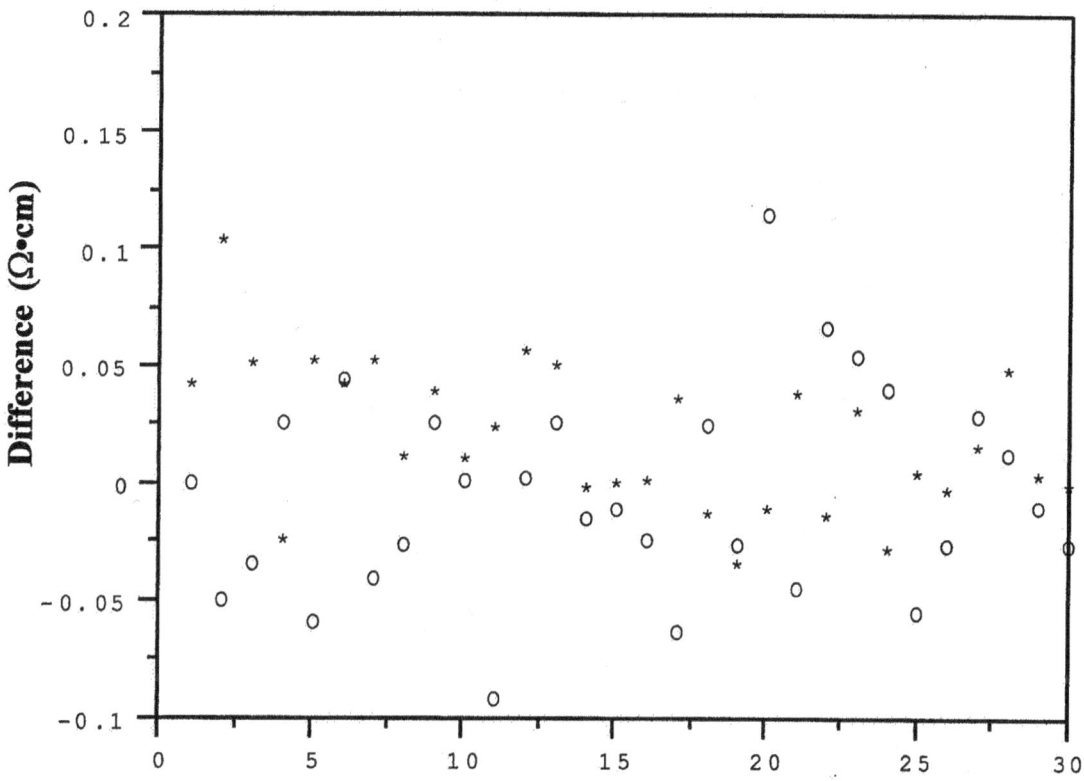

Measurement Number for 5 Wafers over 6 Days Each

Figure 3. Differences between wiring configurations b1 and b2. Five wafers in random order over each of 6 days, with probe SRM1, Ω·cm.

Legend: O = pre-certification; * = post-certification

3.2 Differences among probes

The probes in the SRM certification are assumed to be a random sample of similar probes. However, certification using a single probe can have a systematic effect on the measurements. For this SRM, the measurements with SRM1 are found to be high relative to measurements with the other probes. Figures 4 and 5 show differences from the mean for each wafer plotted by probe. The systematic nature of these differences argues that the measurements made with SRM1 (identified by the number 1 in the plots) should be corrected to the average of the five probes based on the pre- and post-certification control measurements.

The estimated correction is calculated as the average of the differences in the table below to be $\hat{C}$ = -0.049 Ω·cm. The standard deviation of the differences is divided by $\sqrt{10}$ to obtain the standard deviation of the correction, s_C = 0.0050 Ω·cm. The correction, $\hat{C}$, is applied to all certified resistivity values, and its standard deviation is taken as a Type A component of uncertainty.

Table 8. Differences between Multi-Probe Average and Probe SRM1 for Each of the Control-Wafers, Ω·cm

Wafer	Pre-certification	Post-certification
20	-0.054	-0.049
40	-0.061	-0.026
60	-0.036	-0.076
80	-0.050	-0.050
100	-0.061	-0.026

Mean difference = -0.049 Ω·cm
Standard deviation, s = 0.0159 Ω·cm
Correction to be applied = -0.049 Ω·cm
Standard deviation of correction, s/$\sqrt{10}$ = 0.005 Ω·cm

Crystal 21566

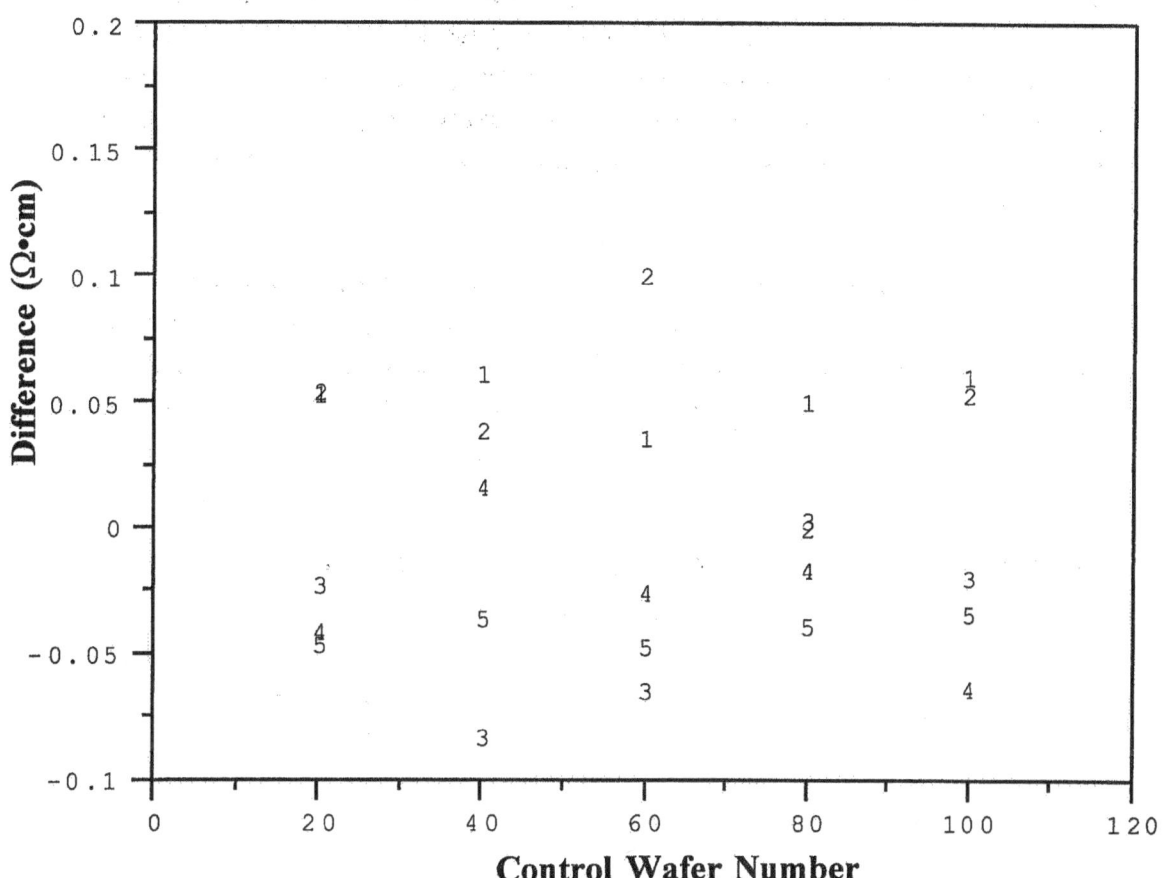

Figure 4. Differences between individual probe responses and multiprobe average, for pre-certification measurements on each of the control-wafers.

Plot symbol code: 1 = SRM1; 2 = 281; 3 = 283; 4 = 2062; 5 = 2362

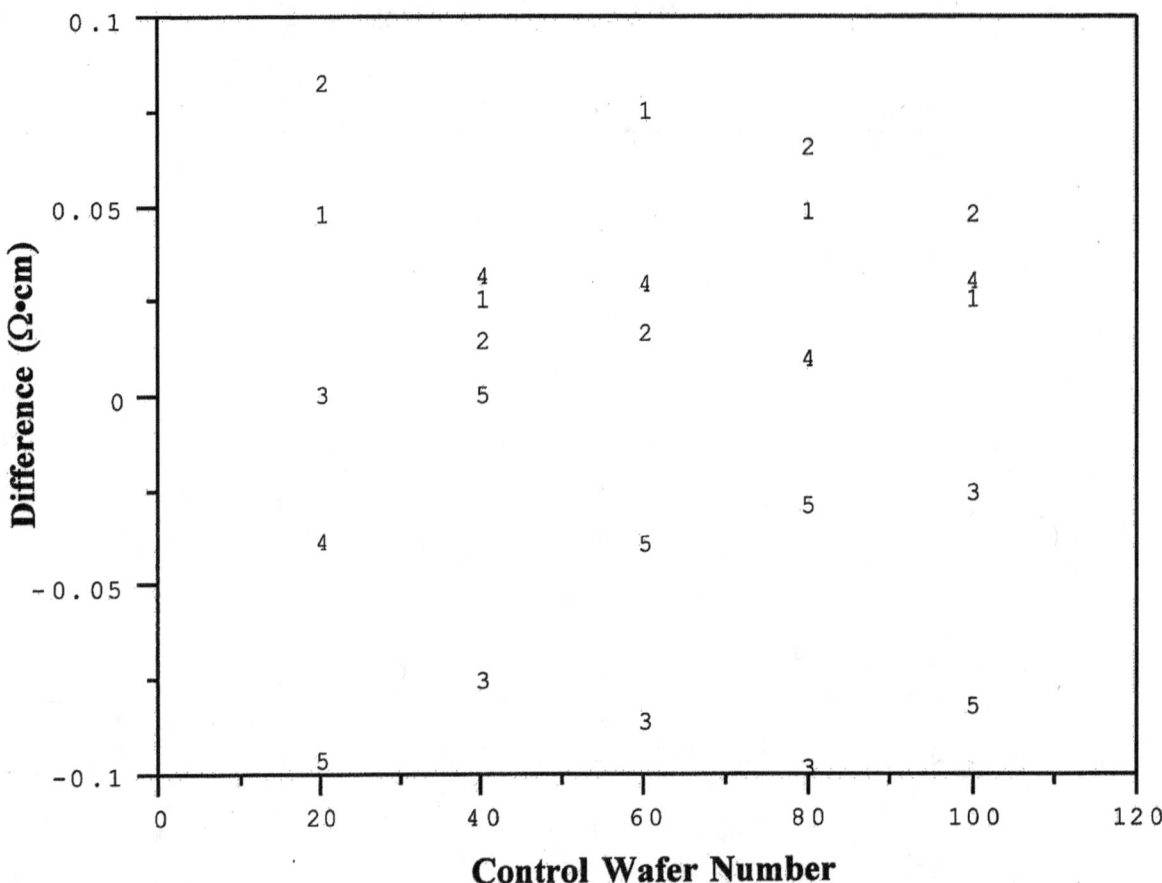

Figure 5. Differences between individual probe responses and multiprobe average, for post-certification measurements on each of the control-wafers.
Plot symbols: 1 = SRM1; 2 = 281; 3 = 283; 4 = 2062; 5 = 2362

3.3 Initial wafer damage

There is evidence from previous as well as present experiments that initial probing may change the surface characteristics of the 200 Ω·cm wafers. The phenomenon is not totally understood nor always consistent, but has displayed itself as an initial drop in resistivity. The resistivity on check-wafer #150 dropped 0.3 Ω·cm after the first day's measurements and then leveled off. For the pre- and post-certification measurements with SRM1, the resistivities always dropped after the first measurement for probe SRM1 (see Fig. 1). The average drop is $\Delta = 0.132$ $\Omega \cdot$cm, and the standard deviation is $s = 0.0427$ $\Omega \cdot$cm. A correction of - $\Delta/2$ would assume an equal probability of initial damage between 0 and $-\Delta$ $\Omega \cdot$cm. However, we choose to apply a correction for this asymmetry not to the data, but rather to the calculation of the uncertainty in Section 1.2. The term Δ is added to the lower limit of the expanded uncertainty. The standard deviation associated with Δ is $s/\sqrt{20}$ $\Omega \cdot$cm or 0.010 $\Omega \cdot$cm, and is treated as a Type A component of uncertainty in the analysis.

Table 9. Drop in Resistivity between First and Second Measurements of Control-Wafers with Probe SRM1, $\Omega \cdot$cm

Wafer	Pre-certification	Post-certification
20	0.086	0.185
40	0.122	0.072
60	0.174	0.122
80	0.177	0.093
100	0.113	0.176

The resistivity dropped after the first measurement (a measurement is the average of six readings at the wafer center) for all five control-wafers in both the pre- and post-certification experiments with probe SRM1, i.e., ten times out of ten possibilities. However, for the other probes, the number of times there was a drop after the first measurement in the same experiments was as follows: 2062 - seven out of ten possibilities; 281 - four out of ten; 2362 - four out of ten; and 283 - six out of ten possibilities. Thus, the effect is stronger for probe SRM1 than for any of the other probes. Plots of the complete data from the pre- and post-certification experiments are given in Figures 6 and 7.

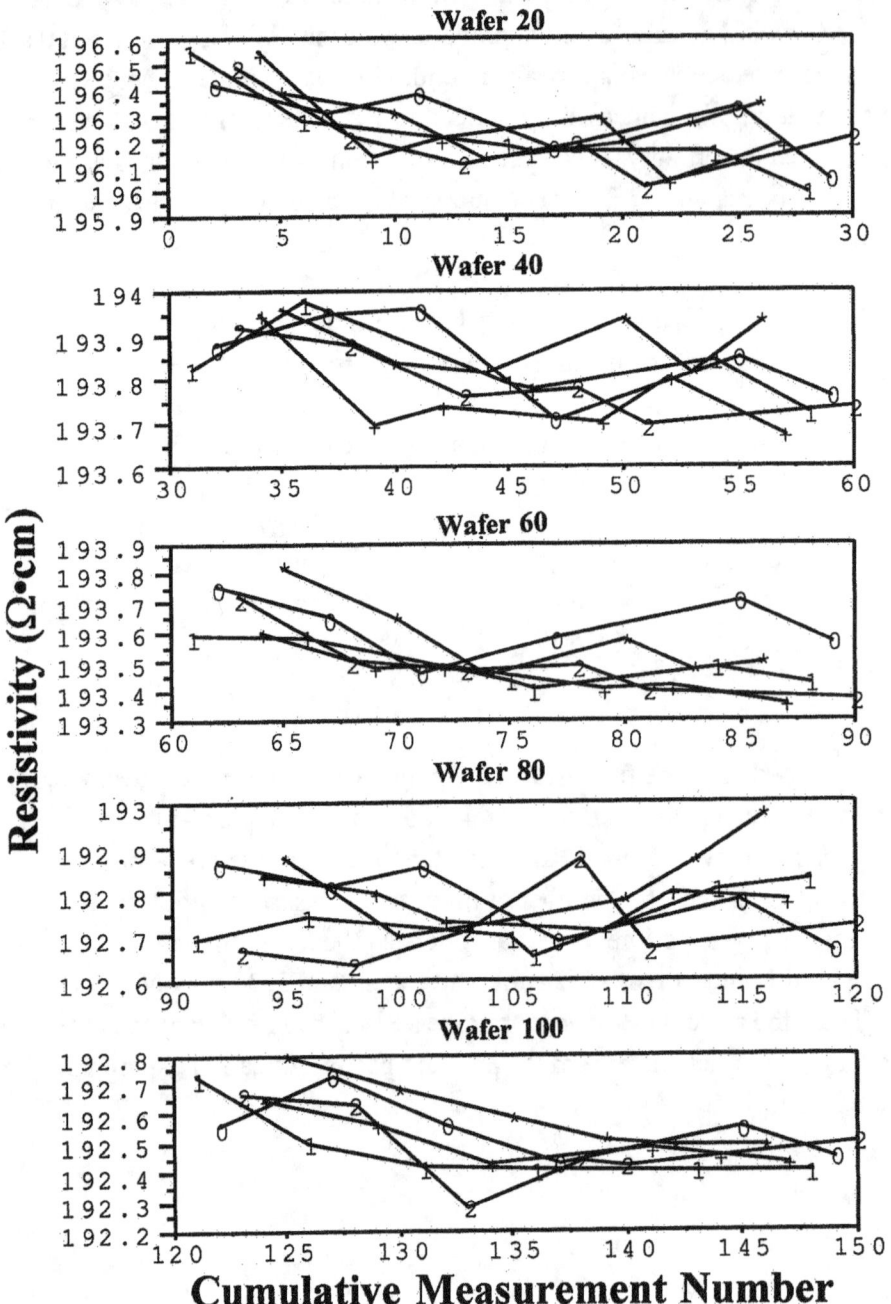

Figure 6. Resistivity (Ω·cm) from pre-certification measurements for five control-wafers from crystal 21566 vs. cumulative measurement run number.

Plot symbol code: 281 = 0; 2062 = 1; 2362 = 2; 283 = +, SRM1 = *

64

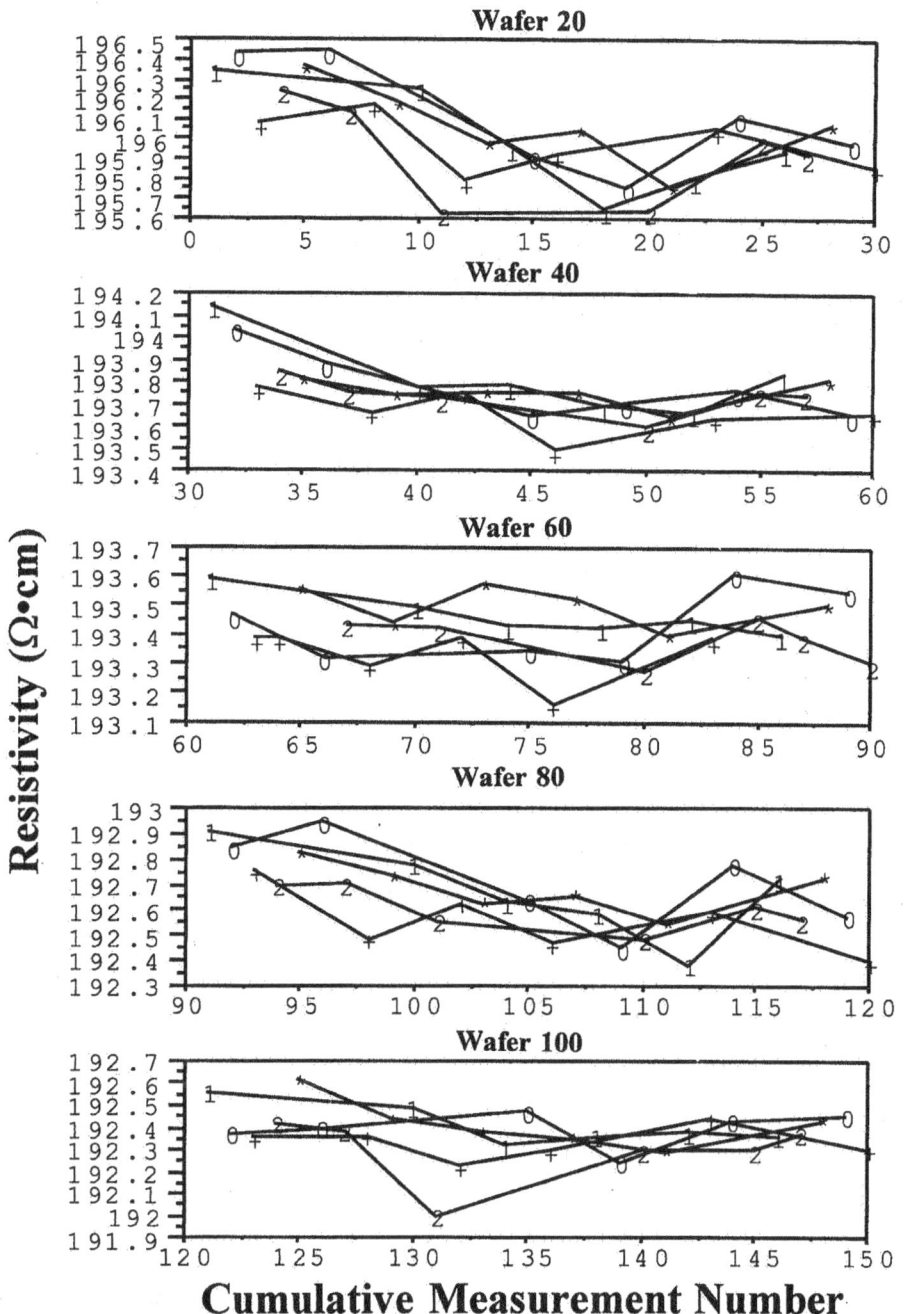

Figure 7. Resistivity ($\Omega \cdot$cm) from post-certification measurements for five control-wafers from crystal 21566 vs. cumulative measurement run number.

Plot symbol code: 281 = 0; 2062 = 1; 2362 = 2; 283 = +, SRM1 = *

Reference:

Graybill, F. A., An Introduction to Linear Statistical Models, Vol. 1 (McGraw-Hill, New York, 1961), pp. 349-351.

Appendix 3. Analysis of Certification Data and Control Experiments for SRM 2541

1. GENERAL COMMENTS AND SUMMARY OF TYPE A STANDARD UNCERTAINTY COMPONENTS

1.1 Introduction

This appendix documents the statistical analysis leading to the certification of wafers from crystal 91905 for SRM 2541. The 130 wafers in this issue have nominal resistivities of 0.01 Ω·cm, and the wafers are assumed to be identical with regard to face. For this issue, the pre- and post-certification measurements were made on opposite faces of each wafer. Certification measurements were made with probe 283.

This appendix includes a summary of the temporal and other components of uncertainty in Section 1.2, and details of the analysis for a systematic bias for probe 283 in Section 2.1. Such a probe-bias calculation was not illustrated in Appendix 2. The analyses of all other effects follow the procedures detailed in Appendix 2. The details are not included here.

1.2 Certified Resistivities and Uncertainties

The averages of six measurements on the 0 mm circle, and individual measurements on the 5 mm and 10 mm circles of each wafer are reported as certified values. No correction is applied for probe or wiring effects.

Only Type A uncertainty evaluation procedures are treated in this appendix, and estimates of all uncertainty components are shown in Table 1. The Type A standard uncertainty for the average resistivity at the wafer center is

$$u_i = \sqrt{\frac{b^2}{3} + s_\gamma^2 + s_\delta^2 + \frac{1}{6}s_\varepsilon^2} = 0.000\ 004\ 2\ \Omega\text{·cm} \ (0.0042\ \text{m}\Omega\text{·cm}) \ .$$

Table 1. Components of Type A Standard Uncertainty for Crystal 91905, SRM 2541 with Probe 283, $\Omega \cdot cm$

Type	Source	Std dev	Estimate
Random	Imprecision of probe 283	s_ϵ	0.000 001 83
Random	Run-to-run measurement variability	s_δ	0.000 001 04
Random	Long-term measurement variability	s_γ	0.000 004 00
Systematic	Uncertainty of zero correction for probe 283 bias	$b/\sqrt{3}$	0.000 000 47

Table 2. Sources of Variation for Crystal 91905, SRM 2541 with Probe 283, $\Omega\cdot$cm

Source of error	Experiment	RMSE [a]	DF [b]	Relationship [c]
Probe imprecision	SRM certifications	0.000 001 70	650	s_ε
	Pre-certification	0.000 002 30	150	
	Post- certification	0.000 002 02	150	
	Check standard	0.000 001 54	105	
	Pooled	0.000 001 83	1055	
Run-to-run	Pre- certification	0.000 001 59	25	$\left(s_\delta^2 + \frac{1}{6}s_\varepsilon^2\right)^{1/2}$
	Post-certification	0.000 001 20	25	
	Check standard	0.000 000 87	20	
	Pooled	0.000 001 28	70	
Long-term	Pre- and post-certification	0.000 004 03	5	$\left(s_\gamma^2 + \frac{1}{6}s_\delta^2 + \frac{1}{36}s_\varepsilon^2\right)^{1/2}$

[a]The root-mean-square error, RMSE, estimates within each source-of-error category are pooled in the table above. Standard deviations associated with the individual effects, namely, imprecision, run-to-run variability, probe variability, and long-term variability, are computed using the relationship shown in the last column, with the results summarized in Table 1 of this Appendix.
[b]Degrees of Freedom.
[c]This column expresses the error components that comprise the pooled value in each "source of error" series of experiments; see reference at the end of Appendix 2.

The Type A standard uncertainty for individual resistivity values on the 5 mm and 10 mm radius circles is

$$u_i = \sqrt{\frac{b^2}{3} + s_\gamma^2 + s_\delta^2 + s_\varepsilon^2} = 0.000\ 004\ 5\ \Omega\cdot\text{cm}\ (0.004\ 5\ \text{m}\Omega\cdot\text{cm})\ .$$

2. SYSTEMATIC EFFECTS

2.1 Bias Effect of Probe 283

There is a small systematic bias for this probe (relative to the average over all probes); the average bias is -0.000 000 68 $\Omega\cdot$cm with a standard deviation of the average of 0.000 000 21 $\Omega\cdot$cm. This bias can be seen in the measurements on the control-wafers, but does not affect the values of the SRMs which are only reported to six places beyond the decimal point. Therefore, the correction is taken to be zero. A conservative assumption is that during the certification the bias could fall somewhere within the limits ±b where b = 0.000 000 82 $\Omega\cdot$cm, and a contribution of b/$\sqrt{3}$ = 0.000 000 47 $\Omega\cdot$cm is included as a systematic component of the Type A standard uncertainty.

Table 3. Bias of Probe 283 Relative to the Average of All Probes, $\Omega\cdot$cm

Wafer	Pre-certification	Post-certification
2	-0.000 000 16	-0.000 000 32
43	-0.000 000 58	-0.000 000 58
44	0.000 000 48	-0.000 001 10
53	-0.000 001 44	-0.000 000 86
144	-0.000 000 94	-0.000 000 26
Mean	-0.000 000 53	-0.000 000 82

69

Appendix 4. Analysis of Certification Data and Control Experiments for SRM 2542

1. GENERAL COMMENTS AND SUMMARY OF TYPE A STANDARD UNCERTAINTY COMPONENTS

1.1 Introduction

This appendix documents the statistical analysis leading to the certification of wafers from crystal 91904 for SRM 2542. The 129 wafers in this issue have nominal resistivities of 0.1 $\Omega \cdot$ cm, and the wafers are assumed to be identical with regard to face. For this issue, the pre- and post-certification measurements were made on opposite faces of each wafer. Certification measurements were made with probe 281.

This appendix includes a summary of the temporal and other components of uncertainty in Section 1.2, as well as the details of analysis of a term due to differences in probe-wiring configurations in Section 2.1. Such a probe-wiring calculation was not illustrated in Appendices 2 or 3. All other analyses follow procedures detailed in preceding appendices.

1.2 Certified Resistivities and Uncertainties

The averages of six measurements on the 0 mm circle, and individual measurements on the 5 mm and 10 mm circles of each wafer, corrected for wiring-configuration bias, are reported as certified values. No correction is applied for probe effect.

Only Type A uncertainty evaluation procedures are treated in this appendix, and estimates of all uncertainty components are shown in Table 1. The Type A standard uncertainty for the average resistivity at the wafer center is

$$u_i = \sqrt{\frac{b^2}{3} + s_{cfig}^2 + s_\gamma^2 + s_\delta^2 + \frac{1}{6}s_\varepsilon^2} = 0.000\ 045\ \Omega \cdot \text{cm} .$$

The Type A standard uncertainty for the individual resistivity values on the 5 mm and 10 mm radius circles is

$$u_i = \sqrt{\frac{b^2}{3} + s_{cfig}^2 + s_\gamma^2 + s_\delta^2 + s_\varepsilon^2} = 0.000\ 072\ \Omega \cdot \text{cm} .$$

Table 1. Components of Type A Standard Uncertainty for Crystal 91904, SRM 2542 with Probe 281, $\Omega \cdot$cm

Type	Source	Std dev	Estimate
Random	Imprecision of probe 281	s_ε	0.000 062
Random	Run-to-run measurement variability	s_δ	0.000 032
Random	Long-term measurement variability	s_γ	0.000 004
Random	Standard deviation of correction for wiring configurations*	s_{cfig}	0.000 011
Systematic	Uncertainty of a zero correction for probe 281 bias	$b/\sqrt{3}$	0.000 016

*A correction of -0.000 037 5 $\Omega \cdot$cm due to wiring-configuration bias is applied to wafer center resistivity data for all wafers.

Table 2. Sources of Variation for Crystal 91904, SRM 2542 with Probe 281, $\Omega\cdot$cm

Source of error	Experiment	RMSE[a]	DF[b]	Relationship[c]
Probe imprecision	SRM certifications	0.000 046	645	
	Pre-certification	0.000 081	150	
	Post- certification	0.000 074	150	
	Check standard	0.000 086	120	
	Pooled	0.000 062	1065	s_ε
Run-to-run	Pre- certification	0.000 028 9	15	
	Post-certification	0.000 042 5	25	
	Check standard	0.000 044 6	23	
	Pooled	0.000 040 5	63	$(s_\delta^2 + \frac{1}{6}s_\varepsilon^2)^{1/2}$
Long-term	Pre- and post-certification	0.000 017	5	
	Pooled	0.000 017	5	$(s_\gamma^2 + \frac{1}{6}s_\delta^2 + \frac{1}{36}s_\varepsilon^2)^{1/2}$

[a]The root-mean-square error, RMSE, estimates within each source-of-error category are pooled in the table above. Standard deviations associated with the individual effects, namely, imprecision, run-to-run variability, probe variability, and long-term variability, are computed using the relationship shown in the last column, with the results summarized in Table 1 of this Appendix.

[b]Degree of Freedom.

[c]This column expresses the error components that comprise the pooled value in each "source of error" series of experiments; see reference at the end of Appendix 2.

2. SYSTEMATIC EFFECTS

2.1 Differences between Wiring Configurations b1 and b2

Differences are found between measurements in configurations b1 and b2. Averages and standard deviations (for the first four days of measurements on each wafer) are shown in Table 3. Rounds 5 and 6 of the pre-certification measurements were found to have been adversely affected by a faulty power supply that was discovered and repaired shortly after the start of wafer certification. Rounds 5 and 6 are omitted from the analysis of the probe-wiring effect for both pre- and post-certification control-wafer data. The t-statistic for testing for a significant difference between wiring configurations b1 and b2 is $t = \sqrt{20}$ Avg/SD. The values of the t-statistic suggest a slight difference between wiring configurations for this SRM. The average difference between the pre- and post-certification measurements is 0.000 075 $\Omega \cdot$cm. A correction of minus one-half this difference, or -0.000 037 5 $\Omega \cdot$cm, is applied to all certification measurements to obtain an average over the two configurations. The standard deviation of the correction,

$$s_{cfig} = \frac{1}{2} \frac{1}{\sqrt{20}} \sqrt{s_1^2 + s_2^2} = 0.000\ 011\ \Omega \cdot cm \ ,$$

where s_1 is the standard deviation from the pre-certification and s_2 is the standard deviation from post-certification measurement, is taken as a component of the Type A standard uncertainty for the process.

Table 3. Average Differences and Standard Deviations
between Wiring Configurations b1 and b2, $\Omega \cdot$cm

| Probe | Pre-certification | | | | Post-certification | | | |
	Avg	SD (s_1)	DF	t	Avg	SD (s_2)	DF	t
281	0.000 085	0.000 064	19	5.9	0.000 065	0.000 072	19	4.0

Appendix 5. Analysis of Certification Data and Control Experiments for SRM 2545

1. GENERAL COMMENTS AND SUMMARY OF TYPE A STANDARD UNCERTAINTY COMPONENTS

1.1 Introduction

This appendix documents the statistical analysis leading to the certification of wafers from crystal 21565, SRM 2545. The 133 wafers in this issue have nominal resistivities of 25 Ω·cm, and the wafers are assumed to be identical with regard to wafer face. For this SRM, the pre- and post-certification measurements were made on opposite faces of each wafer. Certification measurements were made with probe 2062.

This appendix includes a summary of the temporal and other components of uncertainty in Section 1.2, as well as details of an analysis for wiring-configuration differences of a form not contained in any of the previous appendices. All other analyses follow procedures detailed in Appendix 2.

1.2 Certified Resistivities and Uncertainties

The averages of six measurements on the 0 mm circle, and individual measurements on the 5 mm and 10 mm circles of each wafer, are reported as certified values. There is no correction for probe effect.

Only Type A uncertainty evaluation procedures are treated in this appendix, and estimates of all uncertainty components are shown in Table 1. The Type A standard uncertainty for the average resistivity at the wafer center is

$$u_i = \left(\frac{a^2}{3} + s_\gamma^2 + s_\delta^2 + \frac{1}{6} s_\varepsilon^2 \right)^{1/2} = 0.008 \ \Omega\text{·cm} .$$

The Type A standard uncertainty for the individual resistivity values on the 5 mm and 10 mm radius circles is

$$u_i = \left(\frac{a^2}{3} + s_\gamma^2 + s_\delta^2 + s_\varepsilon^2 \right)^{1/2} = 0.015 \ \Omega\text{·cm} .$$

Table 1. Components of Type A Standard Uncertainty for Crystal 21565, SRM 2545 with Probe 2062, $\Omega \cdot$cm

Type	Source	Std dev	Estimate
Random	Imprecision of probe 2062	s_ε	0.014 14
Random	Run-to-run measurement variability	s_δ	0.003 31
Random	Long-term measurement variability	s_γ	0.003 01
Systematic	Uncertainty of a zero correction for differences between wiring configurations	$a/\sqrt{3}$	0.002 89

Table 2. Sources of Variation for Crystal 21565, SRM 2545 with Probe 2062, $\Omega\cdot cm$

Source of error	Experiment	RMSE[a]	DF[b]	Relationship[c]
Probe imprecision	SRM certifications	0.014 93	650	s_ε
	Pre-certification	0.011 32	150	
	Post-certification	0.014 67	150	
	Check standard	0.012 04	120	
	Pooled	0.014 14	1070	
Run-to-run	Pre-certification	0.006 968	25	
	Post-certification	0.004 588	25	$\left(s_\delta^2 + \frac{1}{6} s_\varepsilon^2\right)^{1/2}$
	Check standard	0.008 056	23	
	Pooled	0.006 655	73	
Long-term	Pre- and post-certification	0.004 057	5	$\left(s_\gamma^2 + \frac{1}{6} s_\delta^2 + \frac{1}{36} s_\varepsilon^2\right)^{1/2}$
	Pooled	0.004 057	5	

[a]The root-mean-square error, RMSE, estimates within each source-of-error category are pooled in the table above. Standard deviations associated with the individual effects, namely, imprecision, run-to-run variability, probe variability, and long-term variability, are computed from the relationships shown in the last column, with the results summarized in Table 1 of this Appendix.

[b]Degrees of Freedom.

[c]This column expresses the error components that comprise the pooled value in each "source of error" series of experiments; see reference at the end of Appendix 2.

2. SYSTEMATIC EFFECTS

2.1 Differences between Wiring Configurations b1 and b2

Differences are found between measurements in configurations b1 and b2. An obvious outlier in the pre-certification measurements on wafer 39 was deleted from the database for the purpose of the analysis. Averages and standard deviations are shown in Table 3. The t-statistic for testing for a significant difference between wiring configurations b1 and b2 is $t = \sqrt{29}$ Avg/SD. The t-statistics suggest a slight difference among wiring configurations for this issue, although the differences are in opposite directions for the pre- and post-certification measurements. With no other information at hand, it is reasonable to assume that during the certification procedure, the difference between wiring configurations could fall somewhere within the limits $\pm a$, where $a = 0.005$ $\Omega \cdot$cm is based on the post-certification average value. It is also reasonable to assume that the best correction is zero, and that the standard uncertainty for the underlying uniform distribution is $a/\sqrt{3}$, or 0.002 89 $\Omega \cdot$cm.

Table 3. Average Differences and Standard Deviations
between Wiring Configurations b1 and b2, $\Omega \cdot$cm

| Probe | Pre-certification | | | | Post-certification | | | |
	Avg	SD	DF	t	Avg	SD	DF	t
2062	-0.003 83	0.005 14	28	-4.0	+ 0.004 89	0.004 00	28	6.6

Appendix 6. Analysis of Certification Data and Control Experiments
for SRM 2546

1. GENERAL COMMENTS AND SUMMARY OF TYPE A STANDARD UNCERTAINTY COMPONENTS

1.1 Introduction

This appendix documents the statistical analysis leading to the certification of wafers from crystal 51939 for SRM 2546. The 130 wafers in this issue have nominal resistivities of 100 $\Omega \cdot$cm, and the wafers are assumed to be identical with regard to face; all measurements were made on the same face of each wafer. All certification measurements were made with probe 2362.

This appendix contains a summary of the temporal and other components of uncertainty in Section 1.2. All analyses of the temporal components of uncertainty for this SRM follow procedures detailed in Appendix 2 for analysis of SRM 2547. Section 2.1 summarizes an analysis of a probe bias correction that follows the procedures used in Appendix 2.

1.2 Certified Resistivities and Uncertainties

The averages of six measurements on the 0 mm circle, and individual measurements on the 5 mm and 10 mm circles of each wafer, corrected for probe #2362 are reported as certified values.

Only Type A uncertainty evaluation procedures are treated in this appendix, and estimates of all uncertainty components are shown in Table 1. The Type A standard uncertainty for the average resistivity at the wafer center is

$$u_i = \left(s_c^2 + s_\gamma^2 + s_\delta^2 + \tfrac{1}{6} s_\varepsilon^2 \right)^{1/2} = 0.036\ \Omega \cdot \text{cm} .$$

The Type A standard uncertainty for individual resistivity values on the 5 mm and 10 mm radius circles is

$$u_i = \left(s_c^2 + s_\gamma^2 + s_\delta^2 + s_\varepsilon^2 \right)^{1/2} = 0.075\ \text{cm} .$$

Table 1. Components of Type A Standard Uncertainty for Wafers from Crystal 51939, SRM 2546 with Probe 2362, $\Omega \cdot cm$

Type	Source	Std dev	Estimate
Random	Imprecision of probe 2362	s_ε	0.0720
Random	Run-to-run measurement variability	s_δ	0.0134
Random	Long-term measurement variability	s_γ	0.0146
Random	Standard deviation of the correction for probe 2362 bias*	s_c	0.0051

*A correction of 0.0393 $\Omega \cdot cm$ due to probe 2362 bias is applied wafer-center resistivity data for all wafers.

Table 2. Sources of Variation for Wafers from Crystal 51939, SRM 2546 with Probe 2362, $\Omega \cdot$cm

Source of error	Experiment	RMSE[a]	DF[b]	Relationship[c]
Probe imprecision	SRM certifications	0.074 6	650	
	Pre- and post-certification	0.071 0	300	s_ε
	Check standard	0.059 6	125	
	Pooled	0.072 0	1075	
Run-to-run	Pre- and post-certification	0.036 2	50	$\left(s_\delta^2 + \frac{1}{6} s_\varepsilon^2\right)^{1/2}$
	Check standard	0.026 8	24	
	Pooled	0.032 3	74	
Long-term	Pre- and post-certification	0.019 7	5	$\left(s_\gamma^2 + \frac{1}{6} s_\delta^2 + \frac{1}{36} s_\varepsilon^2\right)^{1/2}$
	Pooled	0.019 7	5	

[a]The root-mean-square error, RMSE, estimates within each source-of-error category are pooled in the table above. Standard deviations associated with the individual effects, namely, imprecision, probe variability, run-to-run variability, and long-term variability, are computed from the relationships shown in the last column, with the results summarized in Table 1 of this Appendix.

[b]Degrees of Freedom.

[c]This column expresses the error components that comprise the pooled value in each "source of error" series of experiments; see reference at the end of Appendix 2.

2. SYSTEMATIC EFFECTS

2.1 Bias Effect of Probe 2362

Differences from the multi-probe mean were found for probe 2362 for each wafer, and are given in Table 3. The estimated correction for this probe over five wafers is $\hat{C} = + 0.0393$ $\Omega \cdot cm$; the standard deviation of this average correction is $s_c = 0.0051$ $\Omega \cdot cm$. The correction, $\hat{C}$, is applied to all certified values, and its standard deviation is taken as a component of the Type A standard uncertainty.

Table 3. Bias of Probe 2362 Relative to the Average
for All Probes, $\Omega \cdot cm$

Wafer#	Pre-certification	Post-certification
138	0.0372	0.0507
139	0.0094	0.0657
140	0.0261	0.0398
141	0.0252	0.0534
142	0.0383	0.0469

Mean Bias, $\hat{C}$	0.0393 $\Omega \cdot cm$
Standard Deviation of Mean	0.0051 $\Omega \cdot cm$

Appendix 7. Analysis of Certification Data and Control Experiments for SRM 2543

1. GENERAL COMMENTS AND SUMMARY OF TYPE A STANDARD UNCERTAINTY COMPONENTS

1.1 Introduction

This appendix documents the statistical analysis leading to the certification of wafers from crystal 91907 for SRM 2543 at 1 Ω·cm. It follows the general procedures outlined in Appendix 2, which documents general certification uncertainty analysis procedures and the results for the first SRM, at 200 Ω·cm, to be certified in this series. In particular, however, the current appendix develops a component of uncertainty for a sensitivity of measured resistivity value to ambient illumination level. This photosensitivity appears to exist in all boron-doped, Czochralski-grown silicon crystals, but was of a sufficiently low level to be negligible in the previously issued resistivity SRMs in this series that used silicon of this type (see Appendix 1). The photosensitivity effect was originally discovered through experiments unrelated to SRM certification, and only after certification measurements had been taken for this SRM (see section 6.2).

The photosensitivity in the crystal used for this SRM has a magnitude that decreases monotonically with increasing wafer serial number. Only wafers with serial numbers greater than 100 (76 wafers from about 125 measured in the initial round of certification measurements) are being issued as SRMs. Control wafers with serial numbers below 100, i.e. #11, #26 and #42, as well as check-standard wafer #35, were used for various aspects of temporal and measurement-condition control experiments and are retained for the uncertainty analysis because they were measured under conditions of constant illumination level. Therefore, photosensitivity had no bearing on the function they served or on the validity of the analysis results derived from their use.

The wafers issued as SRMs are assumed to be identical with regard to the two wafer faces, and the wafer face used for certification measurements was chosen at random with respect to the growth direction of the crystal. Certification measurements were made with a single probe having serial number 283.

Section 1.2 summarizes the Type A standard uncertainty for SRM 2543. Tables 1 and 2 give an executive summary of the terms that contribute to the Type A standard uncertainty. The details of the calculation of the component terms are given in subsequent sections. Analysis of measurements for possible correction terms is covered in section 3. No correction to measurement values for choice of probe used, or for illumination level was required.

However, a correction for choice of probe wiring configuration was necessary and was applied to all measurements on certified SRM wafers.

1.2 Certified Resistivities and Uncertainties

The average of six measurements at the center of each wafer, corrected for bias of the probe wiring configuration used for the certification measurements, is reported as a certified resistivity value. The Type A standard uncertainty associated with the certified value at the wafer center is:

$$u_i = \sqrt{\frac{c^2}{3} + \frac{b^2}{3} + s_{cfig}^2 + s_\gamma^2 + s_\delta^2 + \frac{1}{6}s_\varepsilon^2} = 0.001\ 72\ \Omega \cdot \text{cm}.$$

Individual measurements on the 5 mm and 10 mm circles for each wafer, corrected for bias of the probe wiring configuration used for the certification measurements, are reported as certified values on the certificates. The Type A standard uncertainty associated with each of these individual certified values is:

$$u_i = \sqrt{\frac{c^2}{3} + \frac{b^2}{3} + s_{cfig}^2 + s_\gamma^2 + s_\delta^2 + s_\varepsilon^2} = 0.001\ 85\ \Omega \cdot \text{cm}.$$

Table 1. Components of Type A Standard Uncertainty for Crystal 91907, SRM 2543, with Probe #283, $\Omega \cdot$cm

Type	Source	Stand. Dev.	Estimate
Random	Imprecision of probe #283	s_ϵ	0.000714
Random	Run-to-run measurement variability	s_δ	0.000192
Random	Long-term measurement variability	s_γ	0.000154
Random	Standard deviation of correction for wiring configurations*	s_{cfg}	0.000058
Systematic	Uncertainty of a zero correction for probe #283 bias	$b/\sqrt{3}$	0.000038
Systematic	Uncertainty of value due to ambient illumination conditions	$c/\sqrt{3}$	0.001682

----

*A correction of -0.000 131 $\Omega \cdot$cm, due to probe wiring configuration differences, is applied to resistivity measurements for all SRM wafers.

Table 2. Sources of Variation for Crystal 91907, SRM 2543, with Probe #283, Ω·cm

Source of error	Experiment	RMSE[a]	DF[b]	Relationship[c]
Probe imprecision	SRM certifications	0.000 541	380	s_ϵ
	Pre-certification control wafer	0.000 897	150	
	Post-certification control wafer	0.000 866	150	
	Check standard wafer	0.000 724	125	
	Pooled	0.000 714	805	
Run-to-run	Pre-certification control wafer	0.000 312	25	$\left(s_\delta^2 + \frac{1}{6}s_\epsilon^2\right)^{1/2}$
	Post-certification control wafer	0.000 336	25	
	Check standard wafer	0.000 395	24	
	Pooled	0.000 349	74	
Long-term	Pre- and post-certification	0.000 210	5	$\left(s_\gamma^2 + \frac{1}{6}s_\delta^2 + \frac{1}{36}s_\epsilon^2\right)^{1/2}$

[a] The individual root-mean-square error estimates (RMSE) within each source-of-error category are pooled in the table above. Except for the experiments to estimate probe imprecision, the RMSE values are comprised of more than one component of variation. Standard deviations associated with the individual effects, namely: imprecision, run-to-run variability, and long term variability, listed in Table 1, are computed from the pooled RMSE values using the relationships in the last column.

[b] Degrees of Freedom.

[c] This column expresses the components of variation that comprise the RMSE values for the experiments in each "source of error" category (see the reference at the end of Appendix 2).

2. RANDOM COMPONENTS OF UNCERTAINTY

Probe imprecision, represented by the standard deviation, s_ϵ, is obtained from a combination of the results of three different experiments: 1) from a pooling of the standard deviations of the six measurements at the wafer center for each of the certified SRM wafers (this value is given as the first entry in Table 2); 2) from a pooling, across control wafers and measurement replications, of the measurements with the certification probe, #283, taken during the pre- and post-certification control wafer measurements (section 2.1); and 3) from the pooled standard deviations of the check-standard measurements that were taken concurrently with SRM certification (section 2.4). Run-to-run measurement imprecision is estimated both from the pre- and post-certification control wafer measurements (section 2.2), and from the measurements on the check-standard wafer (section 2.4). Long-term imprecision is estimated from the control wafer measurements (section 2.3).

2.1 Probe Imprecision from the Pre- and Post-Certification Control Wafer Measurements

The standard deviation, s_ϵ, from six measurements at the center of the control wafers gives an estimate, with five degrees of freedom, of the precision for each probe. The pooled values of such standard deviations, over the six runs on each of five control wafers, are shown in Table 3. The pre- and post-certification standard deviations for probe #283 with configuration b1 appear as the probe imprecision RMSE entries in Table 2.

Table 3. Probe Imprecision Standard Deviations, Each with 150 Degrees of Freedom, after Pooling over Six Runs on Five Control Wafers of Crystal 91907, $\Omega \cdot cm$

Probe	Pre-certification		Post-certification	
	Config. b1	Config. b2	Config. b1	Config. b2
SRM1	0.000 934	0.001 619	0.000 763	0.001 079
281	0.000 767	0.000 878	0.000 748	0.000 872
283	**0.000 897**	**0.000 981**	**0.000 866**	**0.000 746**
2062	0.000 908	0.001 793	0.000 799	0.001 497
2362	0.001 129	0.000 788	0.001 183	0.000 816

2.2 Run-to-Run Variability from Pre-and Post-Certification Control Wafer Measurements

Run-to-run variability for probe 283 is shown in Figure 1 where pre- and post-certification measurements are plotted for each control wafer. There is no evidence of change or drift in the process. Standard deviations and averages computed from the six repetitions with each probe on each wafer are shown in Table 4 for all probes used in the control experiments. The pooled standard deviations, 0.000 3123 Ω·cm and 0.000 3363 Ω·cm, for probe #283 appear as the run-to-run RMSE entries in Table 2. They incorporate both inherent probe imprecision and run-to-run measurement error as shown in the relationship column of Table 2.

Table 4. Run-to-Run Variability for Crystal 91907 Control Wafers Averages and Standard Deviations for Six Runs, Ω·cm

Wafer	Probe	Pre-certification		Post-certification		Difference
		Resistivity	Standard Dev.	Resistivity	Standard Dev.	(Pre.– Post.)
11	SRM1	1.073 76	0.000 243 6	1.073 94	0.000 355 0	- 0.000 18
26	SRM1	1.060 98	0.000 628 3	1.060 74	0.000 230 9	0.000 24
42	SRM1	1.046 49	0.000 341 5	1.046 63	0.000 302 5	- 0.000 14
131	SRM1	0.991 54	0.000 274 6	0.991 62	0.000 173 6	- 0.000 08
208	SRM1	0.962 49	0.000 212 2	0.962 34	0.000 259 0	0.000 15
11	281	1.073 44	0.000 405 5	1.073 50	0.000 265 1	- 0.000 06
26	281	1.060 73	0.000 266 8	1.060 63	0.000 174 1	0.000 10
42	281	1.046 06	0.000 457 3	1.046 22	0.000 315 9	- 0.000 16
131	281	0.991 46	0.000 312 3	0.991 34	0.000 497 8	0.000 12
208	281	0.962 07	0.000 414 6	0.962 36	0.000 194 2	- 0.000 29
11	**283**	**1.073 28**	**0.000 294 0**	**1.073 26**	**0.000 636 0**	**0.000 02**
26	**283**	**1.060 48**	**0.000 244 1**	**1.060 70**	**0.000 251 3**	**- 0.000 22**
42	**283**	**1.046 09**	**0.000 369 9**	**1.046 27**	**0.000 148 8**	**- 0.000 17**
131	**283**	**0.991 12**	**0.000 328 3**	**0.991 60**	**0.000 140 4**	**- 0.000 48**
208	**283**	**0.961 96**	**0.000 314 1**	**0.962 32**	**0.000 236 8**	**- 0.000 36**
11	2062	1.072 90	0.000 477 0	1.073 28	0.000 326 2	- 0.000 38
26	2062	1.060 63	0.000 305 4	1.060 49	0.000 509 5	0.000 14
42	2062	1.045 84	0.000 399 2	1.045 85	0.000 166 3	- 0.000 02
131	2062	0.991 02	0.000 447 2	0.991 33	0.000 405 8	- 0.000 31
208	2062	0.961 65	0.000 406 5	0.961 77	0.000 751 0	- 0.000 12
11	2362	1.072 85	0.000 349 4	1.073 24	0.000 482 3	- 0.000 39
26	2362	1.060 08	0.000 352 7	1.060 51	0.000 518 5	- 0.000 43
42	2362	1.045 88	0.000 650 7	1.045 99	0.000 263 8	- 0.000 11
131	2362	0.990 81	0.000 621 5	0.991 32	0.000 455 7	- 0.000 50
208	2362	0.961 75	0.000 180 8	0.961 87	0.000 493 8	- 0.000 11
Probe 283 (pooled across wafers)			**0.000 312 3**		**0.000 336 3**	

87

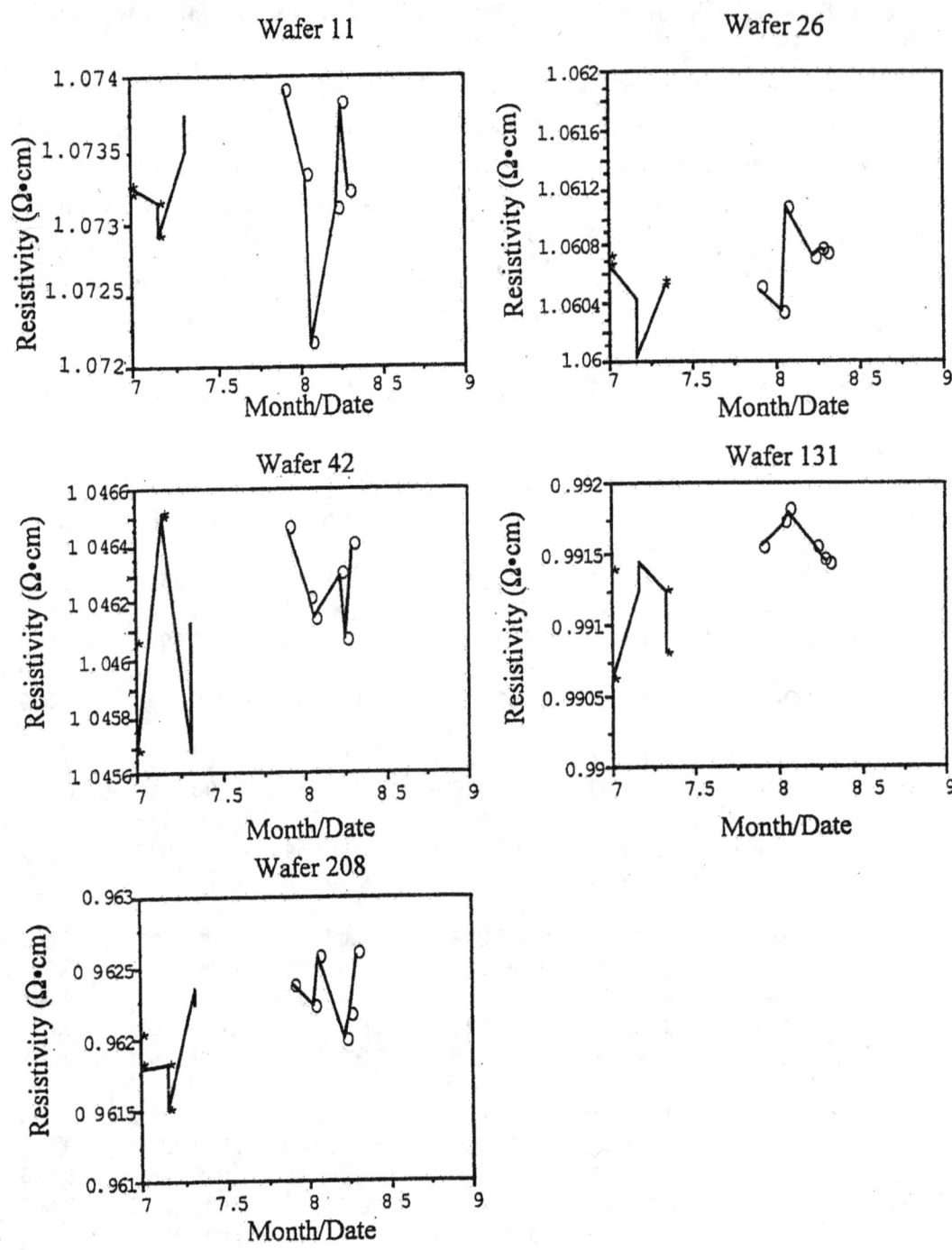

Figure 1. Resistivity (Ω·cm), with probe #283, for five control wafers from crystal 91907 plotted vs. month/date of measurement, and showing consistency obtained both within and between and the pre- and post-certification, (*) and (o) plot symbols, control measurements.

2.3 Long-term Measurement Variability of Control-Wafer Measurements with Probe #283

Table 5 shows averages and standard deviations computed from six runs (replications) on each control wafer with probe #283. The differences listed are assumed to be the result of a long-term component of measurement error. The standard deviations of the differences incorporate probe imprecision, run-to-run variation, and long-term variability as shown in the relationship column of Table 2. The standard deviation resulting from pooling across control wafers is the value shown as the long-term RMSE entry in Table 2.

Table 5. Long-Term Component of Uncertainty for Crystal 91907 Control Wafers with Probe 283, $\Omega \cdot cm$

Wafer	Pre-cert. Average	Post-cert. Average	Difference	Stand. Dev.	DF
11	1.073 28	1.073 26	0.000 02	0.000 014	1
26	1.060 48	1.060 70	-0.000 22	0.000 156	1
42	1.046 09	1.046 27	-0.000 17	0.000 127	1
131	0.991 12	0.991 60	-0.000 48	0.000 339	1
208	0.961 96	0.962 32	-0.000 36	0.000 255	1

| Standard deviation after pooling across control wafers | | | | 0.000 210 | 5 |

2.4 Check-Standard Measurements

Twenty-five measurement runs (of six wafer-center measurements each) were made with probe #283, on check-standard wafer #035, over the course of the SRM wafer certification, a period of five weeks. Run-to-run variations in the measurement process are shown in Figure 2. The standard deviations of the 25 individual measurement runs were pooled to give a value of 0.000 724 $\Omega \cdot cm$ with 125 degrees of freedom. This pooled estimate is given in Table 2 as the RMSE of the probe imprecision from check standard measurements. Also given in Table 2 is the run-to-run standard deviation, 0.000 349 $\Omega \cdot cm$, of the average values from the 25 measurement runs.

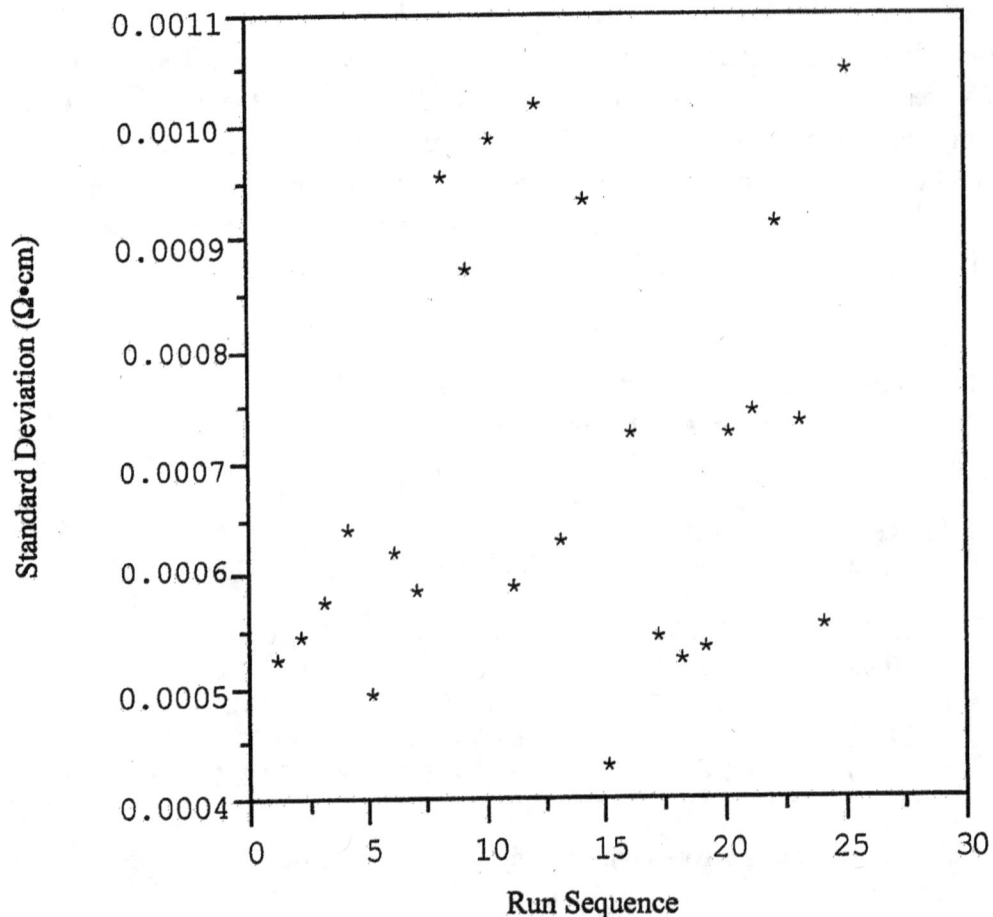

Figure 2. Standard deviation (Ω•cm), for resistivity measurement runs made with probe #283 on check standard wafer #035 during the course of the certification measurements.

3. SYSTEMATIC EFFECT COMPONENTS OF UNCERTAINTY

3.1 Effect of Using Probe #283 for Certification

Probe #283 is shown as the symbol "3" in Figure 3 which plots the offset, or bias, of each probe compared to the multiprobe average. These data are also summarized in Table 6. There is a shift in the direction of the bias of probe #283 from the pre-certification measurements to the post-certification measurements. Therefore, any correction for bias of probe #283 is taken to be zero. A conservative assumption is that during SRM certification the functional bias could have fallen somewhere within the limits $\pm$ b where b = 0.000 0652 Ω·cm; a standard uncertainty of $b\sqrt{3}$ = 0.000 038 Ω·cm is included as a systematic component of the uncertainty.

Table 6. Difference (Bias) from Multi-probe Grand Mean for Each
Probe and Each Control Wafer, Ω·cm.

Wafer	Probe	Pre-certification	Post-certification
11	SRM1	0.000 514 0	0.000 496 0
11	281	0.000 194 0	0.000 056 0
11	**283**	**0.000 034 0**	**-0.000 184 1**
11	2062	-0.000 345 9	-0.000 164 0
11	2362	-0.000 396 0	-0.000 204 0
26	SRM1	0.000 399 9	0.000 126 0
26	281	0.000 150 0	0.000 016 0
26	**283**	**-0.000 100 0**	**0.000 086 1**
26	2062	0.000 049 9	-0.000 124 0
26	2362	-0.000 500 0	-0.000 104 0
42	SRM1	0.000 418 1	0.000 438 1
42	281	-0.000 011 9	0.000 028 0
42	**283**	**0.000 018 1**	**0.000 078 1**
42	2062	-0.000 231 9	-0.000 341 9
42	2362	- 0.000 191 9	-0.000 201 9
131	SRM1	0.000 349 9	0.000 178 0
131	281	0.000 269 9	-0.000 102 0
131	**283**	**- 0.000 070 1**	**0.000 158 0**
131	2062	- 0.000 170 1	-0.000 112 0
131	2362	- 0.000 380 1	-0.000 122 0
208	SRM1	0.000 506 0	0.000 207 9
208	281	0.000 085 9	0.000 227 9
208	**283**	**- 0.000 024 0**	**0.000 187 9**
208	2062	- 0.000 334 0	-0.000 362 1
208	2362	- 0.000 234 1	-0.000 262 1
Probe 283 (average)		- 0.000 028 4	+0.000 065 2

91

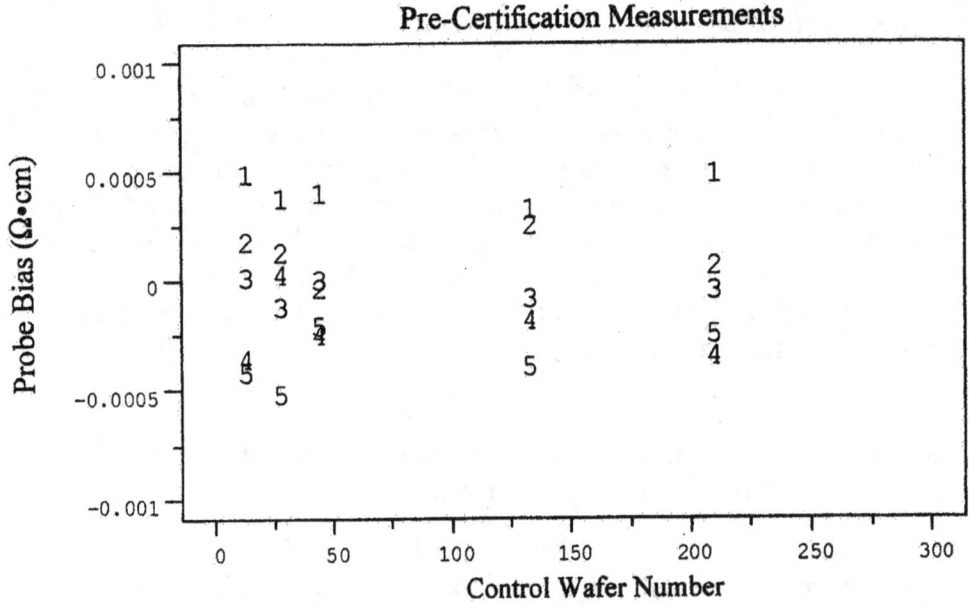

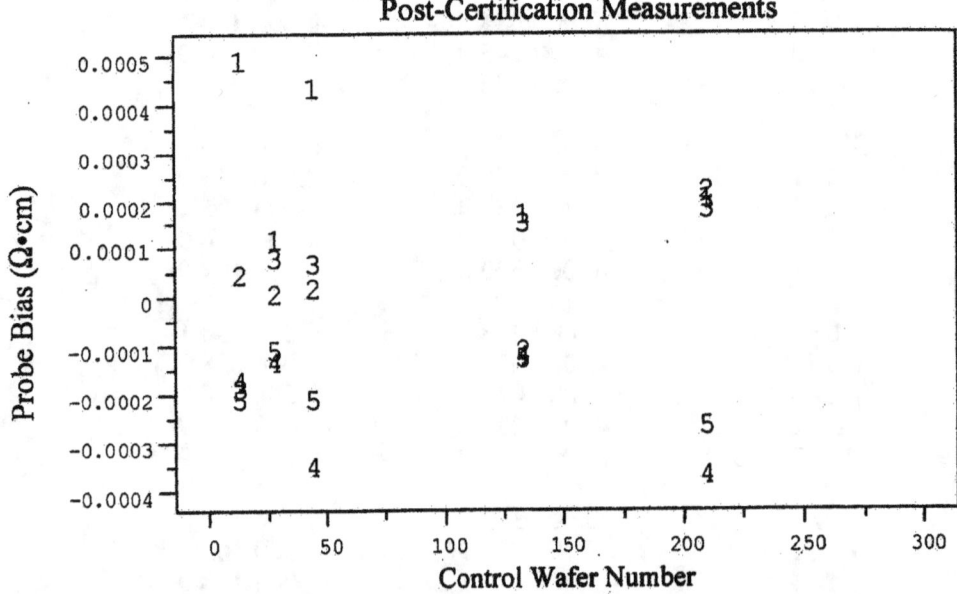

Figure 3. Bias, in $\Omega \cdot$cm, of individual probes, relative to the multiprobe average value for each of five control wafers during the pre- and post-certification control measurements; probe # 283 is symbol 3.

3.2 Difference Between Wiring Configurations b1 & b2

Differences between measurements in wiring configurations b1 & b2 are shown in
Figure 4. Averages and standard deviations are shown in Table 7 and summarized in
Table 8. The t-statistic for testing for a signficant difference between wiring configurations
b1 & b2 is t = $\sqrt{30}$ Avg/SD. The plots and t-statistics suggest a slight difference among
wiring configurations for this batch of SRM wafers. The average difference between the
pre- and post-measurements in configurations b1 and b2 is 0.000 262 Ω·cm. A correction of
minus one-half this difference, or - 0.000 131 Ω·cm, is applied to all certification
measurements to obtain an average over the two configurations. The standard deviation of
the correction is:

$$s_{cfig} = \frac{1}{2} \frac{1}{\sqrt{30}} \sqrt{s_{b1}^2 + s_{b2}^2} = 0.000\ 058\ \Omega\text{·cm}.$$

Table 7. Differences Between Wiring Configurations b1 & b2 for Six Days of
Control-Wafer Measurements with Probe #283, Ω·cm

Wafer	Pre-certification	Post-certification
11	0.000 28	0.000 52
11	0.000 37	- 0.000 10
11	-0.000 13	- 0.000 09
11	0.000 12	- 0.000 17
11	0.000 38	0.000 35
11	0.001 55	0.000 16
26	0.000 57	0.000 29
26	-0.000 03	0.000 11
26	0.000 03	0.001 40
26	-0.000 41	- 0.000 11
26	-0.000 60	0.000 35
26	0.000 35	0.000 28
42	0.000 32	0.000 48
42	0.000 65	0.000 71
42	-0.000 39	0.000 66
42	0.000 86	0.000 18
42	-0.000 47	- 0.000 42
42	0.000 88	0.000 14

131	0.000 49	0.000 66
131	-0.000 03	0.000 61
131	0.000 02	0.001 26
131	0.000 42	0.000 03
131	0.000 23	0.000 33
131	-0.000 92	0.000 06
208	-0.000 29	0.000 30
208	0.000 30	0.000 56
208	0.000 25	0.000 73
208	0.000 18	-0.000 19
208	0.000 26	0.000 30
208	0.000 74	0.000 36
Average	0.000 199	0.000 326
Standard Dev.	0.000 498	0.000 402
DF	29	29

Table 8. Average Differences between Wiring Configurations b1 & b2
for Probe #283, $\Omega\cdot$cm

	Pre-certification				Post-certification			
Probe	Average	Stand. Dev.	DF	t	Average	Stand. Dev.	DF	t
283	0.000 199	0.000 498	29	2.2	0 .000 326	0.000 402	29	4.4

94

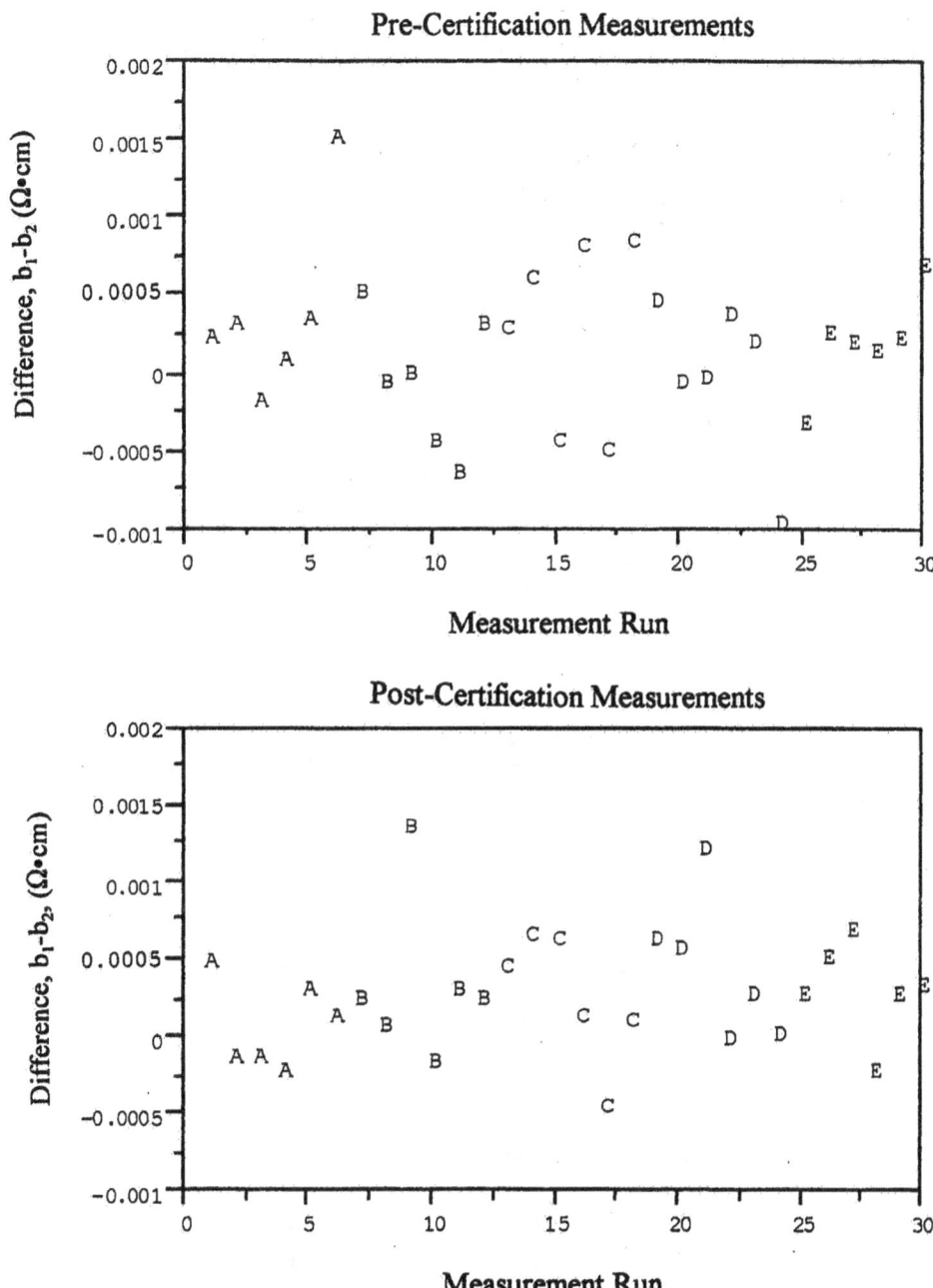

Figure 4. Differences, Ω·cm, between wiring configurations b1 and b2 for six measurements on each of five control wafers, A to E.

95

3.4 Differences Caused by Lighting Conditions

SRM 2543 is unlike the other SRMs in the series 2541-2547 in that the measured resistivity values are photo-sensitive. The full change in resistivity between light and darkened room conditions takes several minutes to occur. The certification measurements were made in, what is termed "standard conditions", i.e. the same ambient fluoroescent room light that was used with the other SRMs. An experiment was performed on 7 wafers from crystal 91907 to evaluate the effect of darkness and brightness on the results. For those wafers, resistivity measurements were made under conditions of: standard illumination, dark-room, and very-bright illumination (bright enough for photosensitivity to saturate). The data are summarized in Tables 9 and 10.

The resulting differences can be seen to be asymmetric: there is a much larger change between standard and dark conditions than there is between standard and very-bright conditions. For wafers with serial numbers higher than those in the table, the photosensitivity decreases somewhat. It is not meaningful to attempt to apply a correction to the as-measured SRM resistivity values to correct the values to either dark or very-bright illumination conditions. Instead, a component of uncertainty is evaluated to account for other possible illumination conditions that might be experienced by the user of SRM 2543. To do this, the larger of the two differences, i.e. that between standard and dark conditions, is used to evaluate the component of uncertainty. Use of data from test wafers in the low end of the SRM wafer range ensures a conservative estimate of the uncertainty to photosensitivity. Under these conditions, the expectation is that under lighting conditions other than standard, the difference of measured resistivity would be within the limits $\pm$ c where c = 0.002 914 $\Omega \cdot$cm, and a component of $c / \sqrt{3} = 0.001\ 682\ \Omega \cdot$cm is included as a systematic component of the uncertainty.

Table 9. Resistivity Values under Standard Illumination and in Dark, and their Difference, $\Omega \cdot$cm

Wafer	Standard Illumination	Dark	Difference
102	0.9981	1.0013	-0.0032
104	1.0095	1.0125	-0.0030
106	1.0233	1.0261	-0.0028
107	1.0047	1.0076	-0.0029
108	0.9991	1.0018	-0.0027
123	1.0057	1.0086	-0.0029
124	0.9985	1.0014	-0.0029
Mean Difference			-0.002 91
Standard Deviation			0.000 157

Table 10. Resistivity Values under Standard Illumination and in Very Bright Ambient, and their Difference, Ω·cm

Wafer	Standard Illumination	Very Bright	Difference
102	0.9983	0.9976	0.0007
104	1.0094	1.0087	0.0007
106	1.0233	1.0225	0.0008
107	1.0047	1.0042	0.0005
108	0.9991	0.9984	0.0007
123	1.0057	1.0050	0.0007
124	0.9985	0.9978	0.0007
Mean Difference			0.000 686
Standard Deviation			0.000 090

Appendix 8. Analysis of Certification Data and Control Experiments For SRM 2544

1. GENERAL COMMENTS AND SUMMARY OF TYPE A STANDARD UNCERTAINTY COMPONENTS

1.1 Introduction.

This appendix documents the statistical analysis leading to the certification of wafers from crystal 29473 for SRM 2544 at 10 $\Omega \cdot$cm. It follows the general procedures outlined in Appendix 2 of this publication. The 144 wafers in this SRM have nominal resistivities of 10 $\Omega \cdot$cm; they are assumed to be identical with regard to wafer face. For this issue, the pre- and post-certification control measurements were made on opposite faces of the control wafers. Certification measurements were made with probe #283.

1.2 Certified Resistivities and Uncertainties.

The averages of six measurements at the wafer centers, and individual measurements on the 5 mm and 10 mm radius circles of each wafer are reported as certified values on the certificates. No correction to measured values needed to be applied due to the choice of probe used for certification, but a correction based on the difference between two probe-wiring configurations is applied to all certified values as discussed in 2.2, and listed in Table 1.

Only Type A evaluations of uncertainty components are treated in this appendix. Estimates of all such uncertainty components are shown in Table 1. The data from the check-standard show degradation in the standard deviation over time. It is assumed that this finding is not symptomatic of degradation of the probe, but rather of debris collecting on the surface of the wafers with measurements over time. However, these data are not used to estimate either probe precision or run-to-run variability.

The Type A standard uncertainty for the average resistivity at the center of each SRM wafer is:

$$u_i = \sqrt{\frac{b^2}{3} + s^2_{cfig} + s^2_\gamma + s^2_\delta + \frac{1}{6}s^2_\varepsilon} = 0.00609 \ \Omega\cdot\text{cm}.$$

The Type A standard uncertainty for individual resistivity values on the 5 mm and 10 mm radius circles is:

$$u_i = \sqrt{\frac{b^2}{3} + s^2_{cfig} + s^2_\gamma + s^2_\delta + s^2_\varepsilon} = 0.00743 \ \Omega\cdot\text{cm}.$$

Table 1. Components of Type A Standard Uncertainty for Crystal 29473, SRM 2544, with Probe #283, $\Omega\cdot$cm

Type	Source	Stand. dev	Estimate
Random	Imprecision of probe #283	s_ε	0.004 662
Random	Run-to-run measurement variability	s_δ	0.001 198
Random	Long-term measurement variability	s_γ	0.005 646
Random	Standard deviation of correction for wiring configurations*	s_{cfig}	0.000 287
Systematic	Uncertainty of a zero correction for probe #283 bias	$b/\sqrt{3}$	0.000 204
Systematic	Uncertainty of value due to ambient illumination conditions		Negligible

* A correction of -0.001 085 $\Omega\cdot$cm, due to probe wiring configuration differences, is applied to the resistivity measurements for all SRM wafers.

100

Table 2. Sources of Variation for Crystal 29473, SRM 2544, with Probe #283, $\Omega \cdot$cm

Source of error	Experiment	RMSE[a]	DF[b]	Relationship[c]
Probe imprecision	SRM certifications	0.004 910	720	
	Pre-certification control wafer	0.003 987	150	s_ε
	Post-certification control wafer	0.004 025	150	
	Pooled	0.004 662	1020	
Run-to-run	Pre- certification	0.002 134	25	
	Post-certification	0.002 359	25	$\left(s_\delta^2 + \frac{1}{6} s_\varepsilon^2\right)^{1/2}$
	Pooled	0.002 249	50	
Long-term	Pre- and post-certification	0.005 720	5	$\left(s_\gamma^2 + \frac{1}{6} s_\delta^2 + \frac{1}{36} s_\varepsilon^2\right)^{1/2}$

[a] The individual root-mean-square error estimates (RMSE) within each source-of-error category are pooled in the table above. Except for the experiments to estimate probe imprecision, the RMSE values are comprised of more than one component of variation. Standard deviations associated with the individual effects, namely, imprecision, run-to-run variability, and long term variability, listed in Table 1 are computed from the pooled RMSE values using the relationships in the last column.

[b] Degrees of Freedom.

[c] This column expresses the components of variation that comprise the RMSE values for the experiments in each "source of error" category (see the reference at the end of Appendix 2).

2. SYSTEMMATIC EFFECTS

2.1 Bias of Probe 283

There is a small bias for the certification probe, #283, (relative to the average over all probes) as shown in Table 3 for each of the control wafers. The differences from the average for all probes are small; they are of both algebraic signs, and sometimes change signs between pre- and post-certification measurements. Therefore, the best value for a correction due to bias is taken to be zero. A conservative assumption is that during certification the bias was within the limits $\pm b$ where $b = 0.000\,353\ \Omega\cdot cm$, the worst case mean bias below, and a standard uncertainty of $b\sqrt{3} = 0.000\,204\ \Omega\cdot cm$ is included as a systematic component of the uncertainty.

Table 3. Bias of Probe #283 Relative to the Average for All Probes, $\Omega\cdot cm$

Wafer	Pre-certification	Post-certification
16	0.000 6742	0.000 4902
32	-0.000 1497	-0.001 7977
75	-0.000 4139	0.000 5331
108	-0.000 2584	-0.000 2708
120	0.000 3242	-0.000 4511
Mean Bias	0.000 3528	-0.000 2993

2.2 Difference Between Wiring Configurations b_1 & b_2

Differences are found between measurements in wiring configurations b_1 & b_2. Averages and standard deviations are shown in Table 4. The t-statistic for testing for a significant difference between wiring configurations is $t = \sqrt{30}$ Avg/SD. The t-statistics show that the difference between wiring configurations for this probe and resistivity level are significant. The average difference between the pre- and post-certification control wafer measurements in configurations b1 and b2 is 0.002 1605 $\Omega\cdot$cm. Certification measurements were taken using configuration b_1 only. A correction of minus one-half this difference, or -0.001 085 $\Omega\cdot$cm, is applied to all certification measurements to report an effective average value over the two wiring configurations. The standard deviation of the correction is:

$$s_{cfig} = \frac{1}{2}\frac{1}{\sqrt{30}}\sqrt{s_{b1}^2 + s_{b2}^2} = 0.000\ 287\ \Omega\cdot\text{cm}.$$

Table 4. Average Differences and Standard Deviations Between Wiring Configurations
b_1 & b_2, $\Omega\cdot$cm

	Pre-certification				Post-certification			
Probe	Average	Standard Dev.	DF	t	Average	Standard Dev.	DF	t
283	0.001 358	0.001 914	29	3.9	0.002 963	0.002 495	29	6.5

Appendix 9. SRM Values after an Extended Period of Time

It is useful to evaluate how closely the original SRM measurements can be reproduced after
extended periods of time since the original certification and control measurements were taken for
each of the SRM levels. To test this, a single set of six measurements was taken in February 1997
at the center of each of the original control wafers used for each of the SRM levels. This was
done with the same probe that was used for the certification measurements of each given SRM
level. None of the probes had been rebuilt or modified since the earliest of the certification
measurements, namely those for SRM 2547, at 200 Ω-cm. However, in the ensuing time, each
probe was used for the control measurements of all subsequent SRM levels, and, in the case of
probe 283, was used as the certification probe for three different SRM levels. As a result, some
wear can be expected on all probes between the time they were first used and the time of the
February 1997 follow-up measurements.

1. Summary of Results

The results are summarized in Table 1 where the entries in the second and fourth columns are the
grand averages from six runs using the probe noted during the pre- or post-certification control
experiments. The entries in the third and fifth columns are the standard deviations, Σ, of the
average values from each of those six runs. The value in column six is the average of six
measurements at the wafer center during a single run in February 1997. The entry in the seventh
column is the standard deviation, σ, of those six individual measurements. Finally, the value in
the last column is the relative difference between the single average value from February 1997
and the grand average, or base-line value, of all 12 runs from the pre- and post-measurement
experiments. Data from pre- and -post measurement experiments are stated as actually acquired.
No correction for probe bias or for configuration bias, such as are identified in some of the
statistical analysis reports as being necessary for the SRM wafers to be issued, was applied.

2. Comments on the Results

For measurements on wafers at 0.01 Ω-cm, 0.1 Ω-cm, 10 Ω-cm, 25 Ω-cm, and 100 Ω-cm,
the latest measurements appear to be randomly above and below the base-line values from the
control experiments. With the exception of wafer #141 at 25 Ω-cm, recent measurements at
those resistivities are all within 0.10% of the base-line values. Measurements on wafers at
1 Ω-cm show a consistent high-side bias of recent values over the base-line results. Because
of the known residual sensitivity of the 1 Ω-cm material to illumination levels, it must be
considered that a difference in illumination levels between that during the latest measurement
and that at the time of the original measurements could be responsible for causing all
measurement differences to be of the same sign. Measurements at 200 Ω-cm also show a
systematic difference between recent and base-line values. In this case, present values are
below the base-line values, in the direction of the shift with remeasurement previously noted.
While this effect may be the dominant cause of the observed shift, average relative humidity
was approximately 45% at the time of the base-line measurements and was approximately 32%
during the latest measurements. In order to put the latest values in perspective, an
additional column has been added to the table for the 200 Ω-cm wafers. This column gives

the two standard deviation (2σ) lower limit value for each wafer, which is calculated from the base-line average value and the lower 2σ uncertainty value given in Appendix 2. It can be seen that the February 1997 values are clearly within the lower 2σ limit for the 200 Ω·cm SRM level.

Table 1. Summary of the Six-Round Grand Averages and Standard Deviations from Pre- and Post-Certification Measurements, Single Round Averages and Standard Deviations from Recent Measurements, and the Percent Changes in Measurement Values

CRYSTAL 91905   Probe 283   Elapsed Time 38 Months

Control Wafer#	Pre-certification ρ_{avg} (Ω·cm)	(Σ,%)	Post-certification ρ_{avg} (Ω·cm)	(Σ,%)	Feb. 1997 ρ_{avg} (Ω·cm)	(σ,%)	Feb 1997 Minus Pre/Post Avg (Difference, %)
002	0.011 286	0.021	0.011 275	0.015	0.011 281	0.046	+0.004
043	0.010 974	0.013	0.010 972	0.014	0.010 970	0.024	-0.027
044	0.010 955	0.010	0.010 949	0.004	0.010 954	0.030	+0.018
053	0.010 923	0.015	0.010 926	0.006	0.010 923	0.023	-0.014
144	0.010 350	0.014	0.010 352	0.012	0.010 352	0.015	+0.010

CRYSTAL 91904   Probe 281   Elapsed Time 19 Months

Control Wafer#	ρ_{avg} (Ω·cm)	(Σ,%)	ρ_{avg} (Ω·cm)	(Σ,%)	ρ_{avg} (Ω·cm)	(σ,%)	(Difference, %)
003	0.114 51	0.137	0.114 59	0.039	0.114 59	0.091	+0.035
066	0.113 88	0.123	0.113 82	0.063	0.113 80	0.110	-0.044
097	0.112 61	0.143	0.112 52	0.016	0.112 56	0.062	-0.004
161	0.104 35	0.146	0.104 33	0.012	0.104 32	0.076	-0.019
287	0.099 61	0.129	0.099 60	0.035	0.099 63	0.047	+0.025

CRYSTAL 91907   Probe 283   Elapsed Time 31 Months

Control Wafer#	ρ_{avg} (Ω·cm)	(Σ,%)	ρ_{avg} (Ω·cm)	(Σ,%)	ρ_{avg} (Ω·cm)	(σ,%)	(Difference, %)
011	1.0733	0.028	1.0733	0.059	1.0745	0.068	+0.110
026	1.0605	0.023	1.0607	0.024	1.0613	0.022	+0.066
042	1.0461	0.035	1.0463	0.014	1.0470	0.078	+0.076
131	0.9911	0.033	0.9916	0.014	0.9916	0.077	+0.025
208	0.9619	0.033	0.9623	0.025	0.9630	0.125	+0.094

Table 1 (cont'd.)

CRYSTAL 29473 Probe 283 Elapsed Time 3 Months

Control Wafer#	Pre-certification ρ_{avg} (Ω·cm)	(Σ,%)	Post-certification ρ_{avg} (Ω·cm)	(Σ,%)	Feb 1997 ρ_{avg} (Ω·cm)	(σ,%)	Feb 1997 Minus Pre/Post Avg (Difference, %)
016	10.085	0.014	10.080	0.033	10.085	0.079	+0.025
032	10.105	0.025	10.096	0.021	10.109	0.049	+0.084
075	10.316	0.029	10.308	0.024	10.309	0.085	-0.029
108	10.186	0.017	10.177	0.020	10.181	0.041	-0.005
120	10.082	0.017	10.073	0.014	10.077	0.056	-0.005

CRYSTAL 21565 Probe 2062 Elapsed Time 29 Months

Control Wafer#	Pre-certification ρ_{avg} (Ω·cm)	(Σ,%)	Post-certification ρ_{avg} (Ω·cm)	(Σ,%)	Feb 1997 ρ_{avg} (Ω·cm)	(σ,%)	Feb 1997 Minus Pre/Post Avg (Difference, %)
017	24.050	0.032	24.046	0.015	24.046	0.104	-0.008
039	24.695	0.029	24.699	0.022	24.701	0.061	+0.016
063	24.509	0.016	24.517	0.011	24.495	0.058	-0.073
103	24.135	0.031	24.142	0.025	24.124	0.044	-0.060
125	24.052	0.032	24.056	0.019	24.054	0.068	+0.001

CRYSTAL 51939 Probe 2362 Elapsed Time 34 Months

Control Wafer#	Pre-certification ρ_{avg} (Ω·cm)	(Σ,%)	Post-certification ρ_{avg} (Ω·cm)	(Σ,%)	Feb 1997 ρ_{avg} (Ω·cm)	(σ,%)	Feb 1997 Minus Pre/Post Avg (Difference, %)
138	95.093	0.038	95.124	0.048	95.131	0.125	+0.024
139	99.306	0.048	99.310	0.022	99.252	0.076	-0.056
140	96.036	0.028	96.077	0.029	96.103	0.072	+0.048
141	101.060	0.023	101.079	0.053	101.277	0.097	+0.205
142	94.215	0.029	94.244	0.039	94.309	0.080	+0.084

CRYSTAL 21566 Probe SRM1 Elapsed Time 54 Months

Control Wafer#	Pre-certification ρ_{avg} (Ω·cm)	(Σ,%)	Post-certification ρ_{avg} (Ω·cm)	(Σ,%)	Feb 1997 ρ_{avg} (Ω·cm)	(σ,%)	Feb 1997 Minus Pre/Post Avg (Difference, %)	2σ Lower Limit
020	196.27	0.050	196.07	0.104	196.05	0.081	-0.061	195.60
040	193.88	0.034	193.76	0.032	193.59	0.102	-0.119	193.39
060	193.57	0.072	193.50	0.036	193.24	0.039	-0.152	193.10
080	192.82	0.054	192.69	0.050	192.35	0.097	-0.210	192.32
100	192.59	0.065	192.42	0.057	192.26	0.074	-0.127	192.07

106

Appendix 10. Analysis of Certification Data and Control Experiments
for SRM 2541, batch 2

1. GENERAL COMMENTS AND SUMMARY OF TYPE A STANDARD UNCERTAINTY COMPONENTS

1.1 Introduction

This appendix documents the statistical analysis leading to the certification of a second batch of 102 wafers from crystal 91905 for SRM 2541, batch 2, at 0.01 • •cm. It is taken from the NIST statistician's Report of Analysis and follows the general procedures outlined in Appendix 3 of this document. That appendix documents general certification uncertainty analysis procedures and the results for the first batch of wafers from this crystal certified for this SRM. In comparison to the uncertainty analysis for that first batch, the various components of uncertainty from a Type A analysis of the check wafer, control wafer and certified SRM wafers for this certification batch will have different numerical values, due, principally, to accumulated changes of operating characteristics of the various probes available for the certification process.

The wafers issued as SRMs are assumed to be identical with regard to the two wafer faces, and the wafer face used for certification measurements was chosen at random with respect to the growth direction of the crystal. Certification measurements were made with a single probe having serial number 283.

Section 1.2 summarizes the Type A standard uncertainty for SRM 2541, batch 2. Tables 1 and 2 give an executive summary of the terms that contribute to the Type A evaluation of standard uncertainty. The details of the calculation of the component terms are given in subsequent sections. Analysis of measurements for possible correction terms is covered in section 3. No correction to measurement values for choice of probe used was necessary. However a correction of   - 0.000 002 14 $\Omega \cdot$cm, due to probe wiring configuration differences, is applied to resistivity measurements for all SRM wafers.

1.2 Certified Resistivities and Uncertainties

The average of six measurements at the center of each wafer, corrected for bias of the probe wiring configuration used for the certification measurements, is reported as a certified resistivity value. The Type A expanded uncertainty associated with the certified value at the wafer center is:

$$U = 2u_i = \sqrt{\frac{b^2}{3} + s_{cfig}^2 + s_\gamma^2 + s_\delta^2 + \frac{1}{6}s_\varepsilon^2} = 0.000\ 003\ 9 \bullet \text{cm} .$$

with a value of 24 for the effective number of degrees of freedom based on the Welch-Satterthwaite formula.

Individual measurements on the 5 mm and 10 mm circles for each wafer, corrected for bias of the probe wiring configuration used for the certification measurements, are reported as certified values on the certificates. The Type A expanded uncertainty associated with each of these individual certified values is:

$$U = 2u_i = \sqrt{\frac{b^2}{3} + s_{cfig}^2 + s_\gamma^2 + s_\delta^2 + s_\varepsilon^2} = 0.000\ 005\ 8 \bullet \text{cm}.$$

with a value of 109 for the effective number of degrees of freedom based on the Welch-Satterthwaite formula.

Table 1. Components of Type A Standard Uncertainty for Crystal 91905, SRM 2541, batch 2, with Probe #283, $\bullet \cdot$cm

Type	Source	Stand. Dev.	Estimate
Random	Imprecision of probe #283	s_ε	0.000 002 32
Random	Run-to-run measurement variability	s_δ	0.000 001 04
Random	Long-term measurement variability	s_γ	0.000 001 17
Random	Standard deviation of correction for wiring configurations*	s_{cfig}	0.000 000 19
Systematic	Uncertainty of a zero correction for probe #283 bias	$b/\sqrt{3}$	0.000 000 64

----

*A correction of -0.000 002 14 Ω·cm, due to probe wiring configuration differences, is applied to resistivity measurements for all SRM wafers.

Table 2. Sources of Variation for Certification of Crystal 91905, SRM 2541, batch 2, with Probe #283, • •cm

Source of error	Experiment	RMSE[a]	DF[b]	Relationship[c]
Probe imprecision	SRM certifications	0.000 001 50	510	
	Pre-certification control wafer	0.000 003 26	150	s_ε
	Post-certification control wafer	0.000 003 05	150	
	Check standard wafer	0.000 002 64	135	
	Pooled	0.000 002 32	945	
Run-to-run	Pre-certification control wafer	0.000 001 28	25	
	Post-certification control wafer	0.000 001 43	25	$\left(s_\delta^2 + \frac{1}{6} s_\varepsilon^2\right)^{1/2}$
	Check standard wafer	0.000 001 50	26	
	Pooled	0.000 001 41	76	
Long-term	Pre- and post-certification	0.000 001 30	5	$\left(s_\gamma^2 + \frac{1}{6} s_\delta^2 + \frac{1}{36} s_\varepsilon^2\right)^{1/2}$

[a] The individual root-mean-square error estimates (RMSE) within each source-of-error category are pooled in the table above. Except for the experiments to estimate probe imprecision, the RMSE values are comprised of more than one component of variation. Standard deviations associated with the individual effects, namely: imprecision, run-to-run variability, and long term variability, listed in Table 1, are computed from the pooled RMSE values using the relationships in the last column.

[b] Degrees of Freedom.

[c] This column expresses the components of variation that comprise the RMSE values for the experiments in each "source of error" category (see the reference at the end of Appendix 2).

2. RANDOM COMPONENTS OF UNCERTAINTY

Probe imprecision, represented by the standard deviation, $s.$, is obtained from a combination of the results of three different experiments: 1) from a pooling of the standard deviations of the six measurements at the wafer center for each of the certified SRM wafers, 2) from a pooling, across control wafers and measurement replications, of the measurements with the certification probe, #283, taken during the pre- and post-certification control wafer measurements, and 3) from the pooled standard deviations of the check-standard measurements that were taken concurrently with SRM certification. Run-to-run measurement imprecision is estimated both from the pre- and post-certification control wafer measurements, and from the measurements on the check-standard wafer. Long-term imprecision is estimated from the control wafer measurements. These components are all summarized in Table 2.

3. SYSTEMATIC EFFECT COMPONENTS OF UNCERTAINTY

3.1 Effect of Using Probe #283 for Certification

The five probes available for the SRM certification are assumed to be a random sample among similar four-point probes. Each is a commercial four-point probe of highest available quality of materials and design. Each has probe pins that have been used for previous measurements and that meet the requirements specified in ASTM Method F-84 for measurements on bulk silicon wafers. However, only one of these probes, #283, was used for actual certification after selection using the criteria for analyzing initial control wafer measurements, as detailed in section 3.1 in the main body of this report.

However, certification using only a single probe can have a small systematic effect on the measurements. From an analysis of the control wafer measurements, there is a small systematic bias for probe # 283 relative to the measurement averages over all probes.
The average bias during those measurements was 0.000 001 13 • ·cm. No correction is made for this negligibly small effect. However, we assume that during certification the probe bias could fall uniformly within the limits ± b where b = 0.000 001 13 • ·cm. A standard uncertainty of b / √3= 0.000 000 64 • ·cm is included as a systematic component of the uncertainty.

3.2 Difference Between Wiring Configurations b1 & b2

In the control wafer experiments prior to, and following certification, measurements were taken with probe # 283 in each of the possible ways of connecting probe wires to achieve the second configuration of the dual configuration measurements (see notation on Fig. 2 of this report). The t-statistic for testing for a signficant difference between wiring configurations b1 & b2 is t = $\sqrt{30}$ Avg/SD. The t-statistics and plots of the data suggest a slight difference among wiring configurations for this batch of SRM wafers. The average difference between the pre- and post-configuration measurements in b1 and b2 is
0.000 004 28 • ·cm. A correction of minus one-half this difference, or - 0.000 002 14 • ·cm, is applied to all certification measurements to obtain an average over the two configurations. The standard deviation of the correction is:

$$s_{cfig} = \frac{1}{4}\frac{1}{\sqrt{30}}\sqrt{s_{b1}^2 + s_{b2}^2} = 0.000\ 000\ 19 \bullet \text{·cm}.$$

Appendix 11. Analysis of Certification Data and Control Experiments
for SRM 2543, batch 2

1. GENERAL COMMENTS AND SUMMARY OF TYPE A STANDARD UNCERTAINTY COMPONENTS

1.1 Introduction

This appendix documents the statistical analysis leading to the certification of a second batch (of about 100) wafers from crystal 91907 for SRM 2543, batch 2, at 1 • •cm. It is taken from the NIST statistician's Report of Analysis and follows the general procedures outlined in Appendix 7 of this document. That appendix documents general certification uncertainty analysis procedures and the results for the first batch of wafers from this crystal certified for this SRM. In comparison to the results for the first batch, the contibution of photosensitivity (see appendix 7 for a detailed discussion) to uncertainty was smaller for the wafers used in batch 2. Also, the various other components of uncertainty from a Type A analysis of check wafer, control wafer and certified SRM wafers will have different numerical values than for batch 1, due, principally, to accumulated changes of operating characteristics of the various probes available for the certification process.

The wafers issued as SRMs are assumed to be identical with regard to the two wafer faces, and the wafer face used for certification measurements was chosen at random with respect to the growth direction of the crystal. Certification measurements were made with a single probe having serial number 283.

Section 1.2 summarizes the Type A standard uncertainty for SRM 2543, batch 2. Tables 1 and 2 give an executive summary of the terms that contribute to the Type A standard uncertainty. Discussion of the calculation of the component terms are given in subsequent sections. Analysis of measurements for possible correction terms is covered in section 3. No correction to measurement values for choice of probe used, or for illumination level is required. However a correction of -0.000 25 Ω·cm, due to probe wiring configuration differences, is applied to resistivity measurements for all SRM wafers from this batch.

1.2 Certified Resistivities and Uncertainties

The average of six measurements at the center of each wafer, corrected for bias of the probe wiring configuration used for the certification measurements, is reported as a certified resistivity value. The Type A expanded uncertainty associated with the certified value at the wafer center is:

$$U = 2\,u_i = \sqrt{\frac{c^2}{3} + \frac{b^2}{3} + s_{cfig}^2 + s_{\gamma}^2 + s_{\delta}^2 + \frac{1}{6}s_{\varepsilon}^2} = 0.0026 \bullet \text{cm} \ .$$

with a value of 25,820 for the effective number of degrees of freedom based on the Welch-Satterthwaite formula.

Individual measurements on the 5 mm and 10 mm circles for each wafer, corrected for bias of the probe wiring configuration used for the certification measurements, are reported as certified values on the certificates. The Type A expanded uncertainty associated with each of these individual certified values is:

$$U = 2\,u_i = \sqrt{\frac{c^2}{3} + \frac{b^2}{3} + s_{cfig}^2 + s_{\gamma}^2 + s_{\delta}^2 + s_{\varepsilon}^2} = 0.0028 \bullet \text{cm}.$$

with a value of 21,512 for the effective number of degrees of freedom based on the Welch-Satterthwaite formula.

Table 1. Components of Type A Standard Uncertainty for Crystal 91907, SRM 2543, batch 2, with Probe #283, Ω·cm

Type	Source	Stand. Dev.	Estimate
Random	Imprecision of probe #283	s_ε	0.000552
Random	Run-to-run measurement variability	s_δ	0.000206
Random	Long-term measurement variability	s_γ	0
Random	Standard deviation of correction for wiring configurations*	s_{cfig}	0.000024
Systematic	Uncertainty of a zero correction for probe #283 bias	$b/\sqrt{3}$	0.000009
Systematic	Uncertainty of value due to ambient illumination conditions	$c/\sqrt{3}$	0.001262

*A correction of -0.000 25 Ω·cm, due to probe wiring configuration differences, is applied to resistivity measurements for all SRM wafers.

Table 2. Sources of Variation for Crystal 91907, SRM 2543, batch 2, with Probe #283, $\cdot$ cm

Source of error	Experiment	RMSE[a]	DF[b]	Relationship[c]
Probe imprecision	SRM certifications	0.000 391	520	
	Pre-certification control wafer	0.000 667	150	
	Post-certification control wafer	0.000 668	150	
	Check standard wafer	0.000 716	175	
	Pooled	0.000 552	995	s_ε
Run-to-run	Pre-certification control wafer	0.000 300	25	
	Post-certification control wafer	0.000 337	25	
	Check standard wafer	0.000 285	34	
	Pooled	0.000 306	84	$\left(s_\delta^2 + \frac{1}{6}s_\varepsilon^2\right)^{1/2}$
Long-term	Pre- and post-certification	0.000 117	5	$\left(s_\gamma^2 + \frac{1}{6}s_\delta^2 + \frac{1}{36}s_\varepsilon^2\right)^{1/2}$

[a] The individual root-mean-square error estimates (RMSE) within each source-of-error category are pooled in the table above. Except for the experiments to estimate probe imprecision, the RMSE values are comprised of more than one component of variation. Standard deviations associated with the individual effects, namely: imprecision, run-to-run variability, and long term variability, listed in Table 1, are computed from the pooled RMSE values using the relationships in the last column.

[b] Degrees of Freedom.

[c] This column expresses the functional relationship of the components of variation that comprise the RMSE values for the experiments in each "source of error" category (see the reference at the end of Appendix 2).

116

2. RANDOM COMPONENTS OF UNCERTAINTY

Probe imprecision, represented by the standard deviation, $s_.$, is obtained from a combination of the results of three different experiments: 1) from a pooling of the standard deviations of the six measurements at the wafer center for each of the certified SRM wafers, 2) from a pooling, across control wafers and measurement replications, of the measurements with the certification probe, #283, taken during the pre- and post-certification control wafer measurements, and 3) from the pooled standard deviations of the check-standard measurements that were taken concurrently with SRM certification. Run-to-run measurement imprecision is obtained both from the pre- and post-certification control wafer measurements, and from the measurements on the check-standard wafer. Long-term imprecision is estimated from the control wafer measurements. These components are all summarized in Table 2.

3. SYSTEMATIC EFFECT COMPONENTS OF UNCERTAINTY

3.1 Effect of Using Probe #283 for Certification

The five probes available for the SRM certification are assumed to be a random sample among similar four-point probes. Each is a commercial four-point probe of highest available quality of materials and design. Each has probe pins that have been used for previous measurements and that meet the requirements specified in ASTM Method F-84 for measurements on bulk silicon wafers. However, only one of these probes, #283, was used for actual certification after selection using the criteria for analysing initial control wafer measurements, as detailed in section 3.1 of this report.

However, certification using only a single probe can have a small systemmatic effect on the measurements. From an analysis of the control wafer measurements, there is a small systematic bias for probe # 283 relative to the measurement averages over all probes. The average bias during those measurements was 0.000015 • •cm. No correction for this negligibly small effect ia applied. However, we assume that during certification the probe bias could fall uniformly within the limits ± b where b = 0.000015 • •cm. A standard uncertainty of b / $\sqrt{3}$= 0.000009 • •cm is included as a systemmatic component of the uncertainty.

3.2 Difference Between Wiring Configurations b1 & b2

In the control wafer experiments prior to, and following certification, measurements were taken with probe # 283 in each of the possible ways of connecting probe wires to achieve the second configuration of the dual configuration measurements (see notation on Fig. 2 of this report). The t-statistic for testing for a signficant difference between wiring configurations b1 & b2 is t = $\sqrt{30}$ Avg/SD. The t-statistics and plots of the data suggest a slight difference among wiring configurations for this batch of SRM wafers. The average difference between the pre- and post-configuration measurements in b1 and b2 is
0.000 506 • •cm. A correction of minus one-half this difference, or - 0.000 253 • •cm, is applied to all certification measurements to obtain an average over the two configurations. The standard deviation of the correction is:

$$s_{cfig} = \frac{1}{4}\frac{1}{\sqrt{30}}\sqrt{s_{b1}^2 + s_{b2}^2} = 0.000\ 024 \cdot \text{•cm.}$$

3.4 Differences Caused by Lighting Conditions

SRM 2543 is unlike the other SRMs in the series 2541-2547 in that the measured resistivity values are photo-sensitive, i.e. they depends on the illumination level on the wafer at the time of, and shortly before, measurement. The full change in resistivity between lit and darkened room conditions takes several minutes to occur. The certification measurements for batch 2 were made in what is termed "standard conditions", i.e. the same ambient fluoroescent room light that was used with the other resistivity level SRMs in this series. An experiment was performed on 4 wafers from the portion of crystal 91907 containing the wafers used for batch 2 to evaluate the effect of darkness and brightness on the results. For those wafers, resistivity measurements were made under conditions of standard illumination, dark-room, and very- bright illumination (bright enough for the photosensitivity effect to saturate in the direction of lowered resistivity).

The resulting differences were asymmetric: there is a much larger change between standard and dark conditions than there is between standard and very-bright conditions. Because of the variety of lighting conditions that may exist in used laboratories, it is not meaningful to attempt to apply a correction to the NIST as-measured SRM resistivity values to correct those values to other illumination conditions. Instead, a component of uncertainty is evaluated to account for the range of possible illumination conditions that might be experienced by the user of SRM 2543. To do this, the larger of the two differences, i.e. that between standard and dark conditions from the 4 wafer test, is used to evaluate the component of uncertainty. The photo-sensitivity was found to decrease with wafer serial number going from the seed end toward the tang end of the starting crystal, and we used data from test wafers in the low end of the serial number range for this batch to ensure a conservative estimate of the uncertainty due to photosensitivity. Under these conditions, the expectation is that under lighting conditions other than standard, the difference of measured resistivity would be within the limits $\pm$ c about the NIST-measured value where c = 0.002 186 • cm, and a component of $c/\sqrt{3}$ = 0.001 262 • cm is included as a systematic component of the uncertainty.

1. GENERAL COMMENTS AND SUMMARY OF TYPE A STANDARD UNCERTAINTY COMPONENTS

1.1 Introduction

This appendix documents the statistical analysis leading to the certification of a second batch (of 40) wafers from crystal 29473 for SRM 2544 at 10 • ·cm. It is taken from the NIST statistician's Report of Analysis and follows the general procedures outlined in Appendix 8 of this document. That appendix documents general certification uncertainty analysis procedures and the results for the first batch of wafers from this crystal certified for this SRM. In comparison to the uncertainty analysis for that first batch, the various components of uncertainty from a Type A analysis of the check wafer, control wafer and certified SRM wafers for this certification batch will have different numerical values, due, principally, to accumulated changes of operating characteristics of the various probes available for the certification process.

The wafers issued as SRMs are assumed to be identical with regard to the two wafer faces, and the wafer face used for certification measurements was chosen at random with respect to the growth direction of the crystal. Certification measurements were made with a single probe having serial number 283.

Section 1.2 summarizes the Type A standard uncertainty for SRM 2543, batch 2. Tables 1 and 2 give an executive summary of the terms that contribute to the Type A standard uncertainty. The details of the calculation of the component terms are given in subsequent sections. Analysis of measurements for possible correction terms is covered in section 3. No correction to measurement values due to probe wiring configuration probe used was necessary. However a correction of -0.000 816 Ω·cm, due to use of probe # 283, as opposed to one of the other available probes, is applied to resistivity measurements for all SRM wafers.

1.2 Certified Resistivities and Uncertainties

The average of six measurements at the center of each wafer, corrected for use of probe # 283 for the certification measurements, is reported as a certified resistivity value. The Type A expanded uncertainty associated with the certified value at the wafer center is:

$$U = 2 u_i = \sqrt{s_c^2 + s_\delta^2 + \frac{1}{6} s_\varepsilon^2} = 0.004\ 06 \cdot \text{cm} \ .$$

with 68 effective degrees of freedom based on the Welch-Satterthwaite approximation.

Individual measurements on the 5 mm and 10 mm circles for each wafer, corrected for bias of the probe wiring configuration used for the certification measurements, are reported as certified values on the certificates. The Type A expanded uncertainty associated with each of these individual certified values is:

$$U = 2 u_i = \sqrt{s_c^2 + s_\delta^2 + s_\varepsilon^2} = 0.009\ 44 \cdot \text{cm}$$

with 607 effective degrees of freedom based on the Welch-Satterthwaite approximation.

Table 1. Components of Type A Standard Uncertainty for Crystal 29473, SRM 2544, batch 2 with Probe #283, $\cdot$ cm

Type	Source		Stand. Dev.	Estimate
Random	Imprecision of probe #283	s_ε		0.004 666
Random	Run-to-run measurement variability	s_δ		0.001 095
Random	Long-term measurement variability	s_γ		0
Random	Standard deviation of correction for wiring configurations	---		None
Random	Uncertainty of correction value applied for use of probe 283*	s_c		0.000 265

*A correction of -0.000 816 Ω·cm, due to use of probe 283 for certification, is applied to resistivity measurements for all SRM wafers.

122

Table 2. Sources of Variation for Certification of Crystal 29473, SRM 2544 , batch 2, with Probe #283, $\Omega \cdot$cm

Source of error	Experiment	RMSE[a]	DF[b]	Relationship[c]
Probe imprecision	SRM certifications	0.003 951	200	
	Pre-certification control wafer	0.004 296	150	
	Post-certification control wafer	0.005 583	150	s_ε
	Check standard wafer	0.005 074	80	
	Pooled	0.004 666	580	
Run-to-run	Pre-certification control wafer	0.002 370	25	
	Post-certification control wafer	0.002 355	25	$\left(s_\delta^2 + \frac{1}{6} s_\varepsilon^2\right)^{1/2}$
	Check standard wafer	0.001 518	15	
	Pooled	0.002 197	65	
Long-term	Pre- and post-certification	0.000 180	5	$\left(s_\gamma^2 + \frac{1}{6} s_\delta^2 + \frac{1}{36} s_\varepsilon^2\right)^{1/2}$

[a] The individual root-mean-square error estimates (RMSE) within each source-of-error category are pooled in the table above. Except for the experiments to estimate probe imprecision, the RMSE values are comprised of more than one component of variation. Standard deviations associated with the individual effects, namely: imprecision, run-to-run variability, and long term variability, listed in Table 1, are computed from the pooled RMSE values using the relationships in the last column.

[b] Degrees of Freedom.

[c] This column expresses the components of variation that comprise the RMSE values for the experiments in each "source of error" category (see the reference at the end of Appendix 2).

2. RANDOM COMPONENTS OF UNCERTAINTY

Probe imprecision, represented by the standard deviation, s., is obtained from a combination of the results of three different experiments: 1) from a pooling of the standard deviations of the six measurements at the wafer center for each of the certified SRM wafers, 2) from a pooling, across control wafers and measurement replications, of the measurements with the certification probe, #283, taken during the pre- and post-certification control wafer measurements, and 3) from the pooled standard deviations of the check-standard measurements that were taken concurrently with SRM certification. Run-to-run measurement imprecision is estimated both from the pre- and post-certification control wafer measurements, and from the measurements on the check-standard wafer. Long-term imprecision is estimated from the control wafer measurements. These components are all summarized in Table 2.

3. SYSTEMATIC EFFECT COMPONENTS OF UNCERTAINTY

3.1 Effect of Using Probe #283 for Certification

The five probes available for the SRM certification are assumed to be a random sample among similar four-point probes. Each is a commercial four-point probe of highest available quality of materials and design. Each has probe pins that have been used for previous measurements and that meet the requirements specified in ASTM Method F-84 for measurements on bulk silicon wafers. However, only one of these probes, #283, was used for actual certification after selection using the criteria for analyzing initial control wafer measurements, as detailed in section 3.1 of the main part of this report.

However, certification using only a single probe can have a small systematic effect on the measurements. From an analysis of the control wafer measurements, there is a small systematic bias for probe # 283 relative to the measurement averages over all probes. The average bias during those measurements was - 0.000 816 • •cm. The uncertainty of this value is the standard deviation of the average bias, or 0.000 265 Ω•cm

3.2 Difference Between Wiring Configurations b1 & b2

In the control wafer experiments prior to, and following certification, measurements were taken with probe # 283 in both of the possible ways of connecting probe wires to achieve the second configuration of the dual configuration measurements (see notation on Fig. 2 of this report). The t-statistic for testing for a significant difference between wiring configurations b1 & b2 is t = $\sqrt{30}$ Avg/SD. Plots and numerical analysis of the data show no difference of statistical significance between these two wiring configurations. There is no correction to measured values needed, and no contribution to uncertainty from this source

Appendix 13. SRM Unit Serial Numbers included in the second certification batches of
SRMs 2541, 2543, 2544* #

SRM 2541, batch 2, SN's:

66	68	71	80	88	91	106	142	148	156
168	184	188	191	201	203	205	212	215	220
229	238	253	256	263	266	267	268	274	277
279	281	287	289	290	291	292	296	298	302
303	304	305	308	309	310	311	312	314	315
316	317	318	319	320	321	322	324	325	326
327	332	333	334	338	340	342	343	344	345
346	349	351	352	353	356	357	358	361	362
365	369	370	371	372	374	376	381	383	384
385	386	388	389	391	392	394	395	396	397

SRM 2543, batch 2, SN's:

62	229	232	234	240	241	245	248	250	254
257	258	259	260	262	268	270	272	275	277
279	285	287	288	291	292	293	294	295	296
297	300	301	302	303	304	305	306	308	310
311	314	317	318	319	321	322	328	336	337
338	340	343	344	349	350	351	353	354	355
357	363	364	366	367	368	369	371	372	373
375	378	379	383	384	385	387	388	393	397
398	399	400	401	405	406	407	408	409	410
411	413	414	417	418	419	422	426	432	433

SRM 2544, batch 2, SN's

211	212	213	214	215	216	218	219	220	221
222	223	224	225	226	227	229	230	231	232
234	235	236	237	238	239	240	241	242	243
244	245	246	247	248	249	250	251	252	253

* Components of Uncertainty for these SRM serial numbers are shown in Tables 7 to 15 (with the designation "b2"). Descriptive summaries of the analyses of the Type A components of uncertainty for the batch 2 certification exercises of these three SRMs are given in Appendices 10, 11, and 12.

All other wafer serial numbers for these three SRMs were certified as part of the original batch (batch 1) of these SRMs, and the uncertainty component entries for the first appearance of these SRMs in tables 7 to 15 apply to those other serial numbers.